Home Seller's Checklist

Other McGraw-Hill Books by Robert Irwin

Home Closing Checklist

Home Renovation Checklist

Home Buyer's Checklist

Tips and Traps When Buying a Condo, Co-op,
  or Townhouse

Tips and Traps When Mortgage Hunting

Buying a Home on the Internet

Pocket Guide for Home Buyers

Tips and Traps When Buying a Home

Tips and Traps When Selling a Home

Tips and Traps for Making Money in Real Estate

Buy, Rent, & Hold: How to Make Money in a "Cold"
  Real Estate Market

How to Find Hidden Real Estate Bargains

The McGraw-Hill Real Estate Handbook

Tips and Traps When Negotiating Real Estate

Tips and Traps When Renovating Your Home

Power Tips for Selling a House for More

How To Get Started In Real Estate Investing

Home Seller's Checklist

Robert Irwin

McGraw-Hill

New York   Chicago   San Francisco   Lisbon   London   Madrid   Mexico City
Milan   New Delhi   San Juan   Seoul   Singapore   Sydney   Toronto

The **McGraw·Hill** Companies

2 3 4 5 6 7 8 9 10   DOC/DOC   0 9 8 7 6 5 4

ISBN 0-07-143215-9

This publication is designed to provide accurate and authoritative information in regard to the subject matter covered. It is sold with the understanding that neither the author nor the publisher is engaged in rendering legal, accounting, futures/securities trading, real estate, or other professional service. If legal advice or other expert assistance is required, the services of a competent professional person should be sought.

> —*From a Declaration of Principles jointly adopted by a Committee of the American Bar Association and a Committee of Publishers*

McGraw-Hill books are available at special quantity discounts to use as premiums and sales promotions, or for use in corporate training programs. For more information, please write to the Director of Special Sales, McGraw-Hill Professional, Two Penn Plaza, New York, NY 10121-2298. Or contact your local bookstore.

 This book is printed on recycled, acid-free paper containing a minimum of 50% recycled, de-inked fiber.

For Leon, we'll all miss you.

Contents

6. Handling the Buyer's Home Inspection   87

7. The Challenge: Counteroffers   99

Acknowledgments

Once again, thanks to the many real estate professionals who provided input for this book. A grateful thanks to those many sellers over the years who provided the questions asked in this book. A special thanks to Jason Benjamin for his work in compiling data, fact checking, and helping with the organization. And, of course, my grateful appreciation to my wife, Reet, for tolerating my endless hours spent typing on the computer.

Preface

Today everyone wants quick, accurate, and short answers to their tough questions. And why shouldn't they? Why should you have to read through an entire book to get to answers that could be contained in a few concise paragraphs?

That's why I wrote this book (and the others like it in this series). If you're selling your house and you want to know about counteroffers or about an "Exclusive Right-To-Sell" listing or about "required disclosures," just turn to those questions, covered in this book, and you'll find the answers.

Of course, if you're just getting started and don't yet know the questions to ask, every chapter thoroughly covers a vital subject you must know when selling your home. You'll learn which questions you should ask yourself, your agent, your lender, or your attorney. And then you'll be given the answers–counteroffers/negotiating, capital gains tax liability, types of listing agreements, or virtually any other subject a seller needs to know. The questions you should ask–and the answers–are here.

This is a book in checklist form. It's easier. And it covers all aspects of selling your home. Yet, if you want, you can still read it cover to cover and explode your knowledge of home selling.

I think you'll find, the *Home Seller's Checklist*, is the only guide you'll need or want to help you successfully sell your property.

Home Seller's Checklist

1

Fixing-up Your Home to Sell

QUESTIONS TO ASK YOURSELF

Do I understand the importance of appearance?

There's an old rule in advertising that goes something like, "Never sell the steak… sell the sizzle." Applying it to real estate it might go, "Never sell the home… sell the castle." You want to be selling more than just wood and plaster. When a potential buyer comes by, you want them to immediately see that your home provides more than simple habitat. It offers comfort, quality, and prestige. And the way you accomplish this is by polishing its appearance. No, you can't turn an old Chevy into a Cadillac. But, you can polish that Chevy to the point where its appearance outshines a dusty, dirty Caddy. The better your home looks, the more likely a buyer is to see its potential… the more likely a buyer is to make an offer.

Have I evaluated the appearance of my home?

If you're like most sellers, you think your home looks pretty good. After all, chances are you've been living in it (unless you've rented it out) and you wouldn't live in a hovel, would you? However, when we see the same thing day in and day out, we tend to overlook the faults—we get used to it. In order to get a better impression of how your home really looks to buyers (the only people you want to impress), you need to have fresh eyes examine it.

Therefore, have a few agents come by and ask them what you need to do to spruce up your home for sale. The agents will be delighted to talk with you and give you their ideas; after all, they're hoping to get the listing. And who better to give an evaluation than people who check out homes every day as part of their work?

Have I checked out the competition?

You're not selling your home in a vacuum. You're in direct competition with every other seller out there. And a word to the wise is, "Know thy competitor." When a buyer comes to see your house, you must understand that he or she has already (or will soon) been looking at perhaps dozens of similar homes. And the big question is, does your house stand out? Does it look better? Or does it look tired and old? Another way to find out is for a weekend or two, become a pretend buyer. Tell an agent you want to learn the market and ask for their help. (As noted above, they'll jump through hoops hoping to get you as a listing client.) See what else is for sale out there. See how it looks. Is your home as sharp? Sharper? If not, get cracking and improve its appearance.

Does my house make a good first impression?

Agents are always talking about "curb appeal." What they really mean are first impressions. When a buyer comes up the street and the agent points out your house, what is the critical judgment instantaneously made in the buyer's mind? Is it, "Yes, I want to live there!" Or is it, "Ugh, what a dump!" Thus, when fixing up your house you should start with that which is most important, those areas that the buyer first sees, the items that contribute to that first look of evaluation. For example, you may not think your lawn or your driveway is nearly as important as that beautiful renovated kitchen you have inside. But the potential buyer doesn't see the kitchen first. It's the lawn and driveway that make the big impact. Remember, you never get a second chance to make a good first impression.

Does my front lawn need replanting?

Be honest. Is your front lawn (assuming you don't have gravel, desert plants, or some other type of front yard which itself needs to be spruced up) in really great shape? Is it really *green*? Or, are there lots of brown spots and bare patches? Is the grass lush and thick? Or does it look like a balding man's head? If your front lawn is less than perfect, you can do something about it. And it doesn't have to cost a lot of money. You can reseed. Or you can have a gardener come in and fertilize and replant dead areas. You can water more frequently. If you really want to go all out, you can have your old lawn removed and replace it with new sod (although that can be expensive). The better your lawn looks, the better impression the front of your home will make. Just keep in mind, however, that unlike painting, which can be completed in a weekend, it can take many weeks to get your lawn into great shape. So start early.

Is my front sidewalk or driveway in good shape?

An agent pulls up with a buyer. The buyer, on the passenger side of the car, steps out. What does he or she step onto? Chances are it's the sidewalk in front of your home (or your driveway). What is the condition of that sidewalk or driveway? Is it covered with mud from runoff after the last rainfall? Is it strewn with toys from where the kids were playing? Is it coated with leaves from that nasty Sycamore tree that thinks it's Fall all year round? Is it cracked and discolored? Take a look yourself. Pretend you're a buyer pulling up for the first time. What kind of an impression does that sidewalk/driveway really make? Remember, you can easily remove toys and debris, sweep leaves, and wash off mud. More difficult are cracks and discolorations. But, working with the city and starting early, you can get a cracked sidewalk fixed, or on your own a bad driveway retarred or concrete repoured. (Yes, it's expensive, but it's usually money well spent.) And there are chemicals commercially available to remove stains. Indeed, it may be an ongoing task to keep that front sidewalk looking good. But, it's something you need to do, if you want to catch the buyer's eye, and in a good way.

Do I have colorful, attractive flowers in front?

Bright flowers add color to any home. Consider, what is an excellent way to brighten up a room in your house, to make it seem hospitable, welcome, inviting? One way is to add fresh flowers. (Which, by the way, is an excellent idea when showing your home.) The same works for the appearance of the front of your house. For under $100, you can go down to your local building supply store and purchase pots of small flowers. Select those that will be especially colorful. If you're not sure, ask the gardening salesperson for those that are compatible with each other and that will add color. (Often they are grouped together under the heading, "color plants.") Plant them in logical places (not helter-skelter) around the front of your home. Good spots would be near the pathway leading to the front door and the corner of the lot, where it would help define it. Water them well and in a week or two, you'll have an assortment of nature's best treasures adorning your house like jewelry. It will make your home a welcome sight to any prospective buyer.

Have I manicured my bushes?

Most homes have some bushes and/or trees in front. Perhaps you were the one who planted them years ago. Or maybe they came with the house when you bought it. However, time has passed and that cute small plant with fern-like branches has grown into a 30-foot palm tree. Those delightful bushy, branchy things have grown into 80-foot pine trees. Or those wonderful flowering azaleas have spread out to cover half the front of your home. You get the idea. What looked good when you moved in, without regular trimming, has done what nature intended it to do — gone forth and multiplied. That, however, doesn't help you. It's no good if a buyer comes to see your home and has to walk through a jungle to get to it. Get some cutters, shears, electric hedge trimmers, or whatever it takes to get control of that front yard. If you're not up to it, then spend a few hundred bucks and have a gardener do it. (Having a professional do it usually leads to professional looking results.) Of course, you don't want to go too far and cut too much. It's like going to the barber. You want a trim, not a crew cut. Sometimes it's helpful to think of the Japanese style of gardening, where every plant, tree, rock, and sand pile is perfectly in place. No, perfection in gardening is not necessary—just a helpful goal for which to aim.

Are the steps leading to my house attractive?

Perhaps you have steps, or maybe it's a cement walkway, or it could be wood planks, or bricks, or whatever. There's always some path leading from the street (or from the driveway) to your front door. Maybe it's short, or it could be long. Regardless, you want it to be clean, and without cracks or detracting marks. Remember, when people walk, they usually keep their heads down to see where they are going and to avoid a misstep. Hence, one of the first things they see close up is the pathway to your front door. If it looks good, it will make a good impression. If it's cracked, muddy, broken, rough (so they stumble on it), or missing (so they are walking through dirt or mud), think what kind of an impression that makes.

Have I painted the front of my house?

What? Paint? No, it's not anathema to a homeowner. Indeed, it's something that needs to be done to every home about once every 5 years. The fact is that paint which is out in the sun, no matter how good the UV filters in it, will get dull over time and eventually flake or even turn to dust. In point of fact, a handsome, brand new paint coat will actually begin to look dull within a year. Studies have revealed, however, that most homeowners paint their homes much less often, sometimes only once every 15 to 17 years. On the other hand, what do you think will influence a buyer to think positively about a property: a dull, old, stained coat of paint? Or a bright, shiny new one? You get the picture. If it's been a year or more since the front of your house was painted, roll up your sleeves, get out the roller and brush, and get to it. Or, for a professional looking job, hire a painter. If you do it yourself, the cost will be minor, perhaps $100 or so for paint and supplies. Or, you can have it done professionally for around $500 to $700 in most areas of the country.

Should I refurbish my front windows?

Few people think about the windows on their house, unless they're broken. Of course, if they're broken (or if the screens are), it goes without saying that you should fix them. But, just as windows are your eyes onto the world outside your home, so too are they what strangers (buyers) look into when they first see your home. Therefore, it's wise to always leave the shades up and the curtains spread apart so potential buyers can see in and get a taste of what to expect inside. It's also a good idea to be sure the windows are spotless, clean both in and out. And finally, it's worth considering the overall appearance of the windows themselves. If your home is over 10 years old, chances are you have aluminum or metal flashing. Or if you have wood, it's taken some wear. On the other hand, almost all modern homes use vinyl windows or aluminum and wood. In short, if the front windows on your house make it look old and dated, it may be time to do something about them. Of course, the easiest thing to do is to paint the flashing. This works particularly well if it's wood. On the other hand, sometimes the only way to make a really good impression is to replace those old windows with modern ones. Many companies, such as Milgard, offer retrofit windows which can be popped into place with a few hours' work. They are, however, somewhat expensive, costing anywhere from $300 to $500 apiece, depending on size. And, of course, for energy efficiency you'll want double-pane and low-E (high insulation value). Yes, it costs a bit of money, but buyers today are savvy and they know the difference. (Which, if you can afford it, means that it will help to replace the windows throughout the rest of the house as well!)

Does the rest of the exterior of my house need work?

Do you have an attractive front door? Is the door handle and lock bright and shiny, or tarnished and dilapidated looking? Are there cobwebs hanging around your front entrance? What about the door light? Is it attractive? These are not questions that I'm asking... they're the questions that buyers will ask... and as a consequence, that you should answer. By all means, if possible, paint or stain your front door. Put on new door handles. Buy a new front door light. Clean up the front entrance of your house. After all, this is the gate to your castle. And if your castle has an ugly outside gate, what will people think of the interior?

Have I avoided harsh colors?

It's kind of like closing the barn doors after the horse escapes, but it is important to take a few minutes to ana-lyze the colors you've put (or are about to put) onto your house. Remember, you're not trying to please yourself here. You're trying to please potential buyers. In other words, while it's very difficult to guess which colors are going to attract most people, it's much easier to deter-mine which colors are going to offend. Harsh, garish col-ors are out. Neutral colors are in. That doesn't mean, however, that you have to stick with beige. Blues, greens, and darker browns and yellows can look attractive. If you're not sure, visit a good paint store and ask for a dec-orator's opinion. Also, if your house is in a homeowner's association, find out if there's an approved color list. It may be that you're encouraged to select certain colors and prohibited from choosing others.

Is the transom solid and clean?

The transom is the casement that forms the bottom of the doorway. It's what you step across when you enter the house. Typically, it's made of metal. However, I can't tell you the number of times I've stepped on the transom only to find that it's broken, cracked, or loose. It can make a visitor slip when trying to enter the house. At best a buyer is going to think, immediately upon entering your home that, "Here's something I need to fix." Spend a few min-utes to check out your transom. Perhaps a few screws, or even a call to a handyman might be in order. It won't cost much, and it could make a big difference. Remember, small things count.

Does the door close well?

Doors easily warp over time. And front doors, which are exposed to the weather, even more so. Of course, if your front door is fiberglass or metal, chances are it will never warp. On the other hand, if it's wood, chances are almost certain that it will. And even if your door doesn't warp, the house may shift causing that door frame to no longer easily fit the door. All of which is to say that if your front door doesn't close well, it's something that the buyer will notice. And it's something that will cause the buyer to say, "Here's another thing I have to fix." When the buyer begins finding things to fix upon just entering the house, he or she will very quickly begin thinking of your home as a "fixer-upper." And those homes only sell at bargain basement prices.

Is the inside of my house roomy?

"Room to roam" is a term that real estate agents frequently use to describe a large lot. However, it also applies to the inside of homes as well. Regardless of the actual size of the home, buyers like to feel open space inside. They like to be able to visualize where their furnishings (not yours) will go. They don't want to be cramped. This all means that it's important that your home not have a stuffed feeling. While you don't want a barren house (which, surprisingly, makes a home look smaller), you also don't want one crammed full of furniture. Therefore, consider thinning out. Often simply moving furniture to the sides of the room and leaving the center empty will do it. In other cases, you may want to remove and store some furniture. Be very sparse with knick-knacks. While you may see them as wonderful possessions, buyers may see them simply as clutter.

Is my carpet clean?

Have your carpets cleaned, especially if they are wall to wall. As noted earlier, buyers new to a home will frequently look down to be sure they don't trip on uneven flooring. The question becomes, what will they see? Are there dirt and stain spots on your carpet? If so, the buyers are thinking that this will soon be their carpet. And will they want to walk barefooted on it? Is it worn? If so, will they feel embarrassed about something so shabby when they entertain their friends? If your carpet is more than a few years old, you should seriously consider replacing it. Yes, carpets are very expensive, often $5000 or more to recarpet even a modest home. But, then again, they make such a big impression that it might be worth it. As an alternative, some sellers will offer a "carpet allowance" to buyers. They'll come right out and admit that their carpeting is old, worn, stained, or otherwise needs replacement. They'll say that whatever price is eventually agreed on, they will credit the seller with an additional sum of money, perhaps $5000, toward new carpet. This way the buyers can pick out their own. It's a little added flourish that might catch the buyer's imagination… and help make a sale. Besides, it's no additional money to you *if* you were planning to replace the carpet anyhow.

Does the interior of my house need painting?

I haven't seen your house, but if you've lived in it for 6 months or more, the answer is probably, "Yes!" The reason is that marks, stains, and scratches accumulate rapidly on walls and woodwork. And they show badly to a buyer. Remember, even though your home is a resale, it's new to a buyer. And buyers want to think of the place they are purchasing as fresh and clean. (No one wants to move into a dirty home.) Therefore, it's good advice to go through and paint as many of the walls as you can in your home. (Ceilings aren't as important, unless you need to match colors, because they seldom get marks on them.) By the way, to save money some people will try to clean walls. However, to my way of thinking, this is far harder than simply repainting.

Is the kitchen modern and airy looking?

The trend these days is big kitchens. This is where the family often will meet. Hence, buyers prefer homes with large kitchens that can easily accommodate several people who may want to stand or sit and carry on a conversation (or work on a computer, or watch television, or whatever). In addition, professional appliances also are the trend as are smooth surfaces (such as tile, marble, or granite), and even smooth stoves (glass surfaced). But, you say, your older home has a smaller kitchen. And your appliances are standalones? You have two alternatives. You can spend around $50,000 to expand your kitchen (assuming you can cannibalize another room to do so), or you can make your small kitchen seem as large as possible. If there's an eating area, put in an undersize table or tiny counter. People don't need a lot of space on which to eat (witness the small tables in most restaurants). And the smaller furniture will make the room seem larger. If you can afford it, replace some of the appliances. Brand new standalone stoves, for example, look so much better than their older counterparts, even from as short a time as 5 years ago. A few thousand dollars judiciously spent in a kitchen can make it a selling point, instead of an embarrassment.

Is my bathroom tidy?

Bathrooms are another important feature to buyers, especially showers. The trend a few years ago was big bathtubs, even whirlpool tubs. But buyers are not dumb and they quickly reason that while they might take a bath half a dozen times a year, they take a shower every day. Hence, the importance of a great shower. Many new homes today feature oversized showers with two or more shower heads. But, you've got teeny little bathrooms? Again, you've got two choices. You can simply go with what you have. Clean and paint that bathroom and hope for the best. Or you can modernize. While building in an extra shower head can cost up to $10,000 (you probably have to rip out walls to do it), there are multiple shower head devices available on the market. These screw into your current shower head and convert it to a double head. With extensions they even reach around to catch both sides of the shower! If you have some extra money to spend, installing a new, colored toilet also can add pizzazz to your bathroom. Just be sure, however, that the footprint of the new fixture is larger than the old, or else you'll need to add new flooring as well. And if you only have one sink in the bathroom, consider adding a second. Modern homes typically have double sinks in the bath. And it might not cost as much as you think, if you already have a large countertop.

Are the windows washed?

The old saw about maids is that they're willing to do any household cleaning, except windows. Why? Because they never get clean! No matter how many times you scrub them, it always seems as though there's some smudge or speck on them. And as a result, the owner is never satisfied. Nevertheless, before you put your house on the market, have your windows cleaned. A buyer looking through a window and seeing only dirt and grime accumulated over the years is going to be impressed, but the wrong way. A professional service often will do it for a few hundred dollars. Or you can do it yourself on a weekend. I've found that using a squeegee works best. And try one of the auto glass canned sprays.

Is the inside of my house light and airy?

Of course it is, you may say. But is it really? Again, don't take your word for it. Get the opinion of someone who's disinterested, such as a neighbor, relative, or friend. Get the opinion of a professional, an agent, who sees houses on a regular basis. It may turn out that what you think is light and airy, others see as dungeon dark. And if it turns out that your home needs some lightening up, don't despair. It's easily accomplished. Sometimes simply removing heavy draperies so light can stream in through the windows is all that's needed. In other cases, simply adding lamps and being sure they're turned on when buyers come by will do. If you really want to get serious, you can always consider some skylights. On the other hand, while lightening up the place is nice, making it "airy" can be more difficult. In moderate climates simply opening the windows so a nice draft can flow through may be enough. In colder climes, keeping the heat up and being sure the furnace has a good filter (to keep dust particles down) will help. In summer in hot climes, make sure the air conditioner works well. (You might need to add refrigerant or repair/replace an ailing unit.) Nothing will turn a buyer off more than to enter a hot house on a hot day or a cold house on a cold day.

Are there any bad smells inside?

Now who would admit to this? Yet, we do live in a house and like it or not, living can generate odors. Further, if there's any moisture, mold can form and it, too, can add to the smell of a home. While you may be immune from the odor of your house because you live there all the time, buyers may notice it immediately. And they may wrinkle up their noses and turn away. If you're not sure about your home, try this experiment. The next time you go away for a few days, close up the house tight as a drum —all windows and doors. Then, when you come back and first enter the place, take a deep breath. Pleasant, clean air? Or musty, dank odor? If you have a smelly house, the first places to check are the easiest —drains and garbage. Sink drains may sometimes emit odor and even a small amount of garbage left inside can get odiferous. After that, it gets harder. Check under sinks for mold (usually black—see below) and get it removed. Wall-to-wall carpeting may generate odor if a vapor barrier was not installed beneath it. Finally, keep a pot of fresh spices brewing on the stove to sweeten the air for buyers. (But, if your house does have a bad smell, don't fail to disclose it, lest buyers discover it after the purchase and come back at you for repair costs.)

Are there any pet odors?

If you don't own a pet, it's unlikely there would be pet odors (although they could be there from previous owners). On the other hand, if you do own a pet, you should assume the odors are there. The most intense come from cats. I love cats (and was saddened when our 18-year-old feline recently died); however, their odor is distinct and strong, particularly from urine. You'd be very lucky if your cat had not, at some time, urinated somewhere inside your house, particularly on carpeting. Dogs and other pets also have odors, again urine being the worst. As noted above, if you're not sure, ask someone who isn't biased. They'll tell you right away. If you have odor coming from urine stains on carpeting, my suggestion is that you replace it and the padding (after thoroughly cleaning the floor underneath). Regardless of the claims of various products, personally I've never found any that adequately remove the smell. And your home's buyer, unless they also happen to have the same kind of pet, will almost surely notice, complain, and demand a clean-up/fix-up. Thus, it's better that you do it now, when you still have control of the home and can decide what price carpeting to replace, than after the buyer moves in and their attorney tells you what price carpeting they want. The same applies to other types of flooring. Wood flooring impregnated with urine also may have to be replaced, and that can be very costly.

Have I checked for black mold?

It seems that all buyers today are keen on avoiding black mold. It's not that most have had a bad experience with it. Indeed, I suspect most have never even encountered it. What they are responding to is media coverage of homeowners who claim to have been sickened by it. Scenes of exterminators clad in white bubble suits, breathing oxygen from tanks, scrubbing the interior of homes have been seen by almost everyone. Understandably, buyers do not want to get caught in that kind of situation. Hence, they will have a professional inspector check your home for black mold and if they find it, will likely either refuse to buy… or demand that you remove it (usually in the most costly way possible). Therefore, I suggest you check for it yourself. I don't mean that you physically look for it, although if you know what to look for and aren't concerned about potential hazards from it, you certainly could. I mean that you hire a pest inspection company (often the same companies that handle termite inspections) to come in and give your house the once over. If they find black mold, they can have it analyzed to determine if it's the common variety or the rare, more toxic type, and they can then suggest methods of removing it. (Sometimes simply replacing the affected material or just spraying with a mild bleach solution is all that it takes.) Don't underestimate the hysteria over black mold. It can wreck the sale of your home.

Have I cleaned up my back and side yards?

It should go without saying that you've removed any debris you might have from your front yard. However,

sometimes homeowners forget about the rest of the property. You might be using one side of the yard as a junk
depot to store old items that should have been thrown
out. Do you have an old appliance out there? A broken
bike? What about old luggage? Sometimes leftover wood
or other materials from a project get dumped around the
yard instead of thrown out. I know that I hate to throw
away any wood pieces thinking that I'll want to use them
for some future, currently indefinable project. Over the
years we can accumulate all sorts of "valuable" items.
But, now that you've decided to sell your home, it's time
to redefine these as trash… and to get rid of them. Just as
we spoke of making the inside of the house look roomy,
we need to do the same thing for the yard. All the
"debris" must go.

Is the landscaping in my yard in good shape?

What? You say you don't have landscaping?! Even if you
don't, but especially if you do, it's important to freshen it
up. Cut everything into shape. (Remember, you want
a "trim," not a "crew-cut.") Replant that lawn. And take a
hint from the front of your house; buy some boxes of col-
orful flowers and plant them at least around the periph-
ery of your yard. Remember, it doesn't cost much to put
nature's beauties in (as long as you allow a few weeks for
growth), and the result can turn a dismal, drab yard into
a flowering garden. Keep up the watering while your
home is on the market and through the escrow process.
(You don't want the buyers to arrive for their final walk-
through just before escrow closes and be greeted by a
yard full of dead and dying plants.)

Do I use my garage for storage?

If you have enough storage space, you're probably the
only one in America who does. I've talked with people
who have 1200-square-foot homes and those who have
12,000-square-foot mansions and no one ever seems to
have enough room to store everything, particularly after
having lived in the home for a few years. As a result,
"things" sometimes get moved into the garage. Yes, you
may be one of those whose garage is as neat and tidy as
their living room. But for most people, there's so much

stuff in the garage that the car can't fit in! Yet, serious buyers will always look at the garage. And if they see it's stuffed with things that are being stored, what's their natural conclusion? It's obviously that your house doesn't have enough storage space, meaning they'll look elsewhere. Thus, you need to clean out the garage. If you're truthful, you'll probably admit that most things in the garage can be thrown out. Many items can be taken to a rented storage locker. And those very few things that you must keep around the house (such as yard tools), can be neatly hung on walls or stuck under a work bench. Take some time to clean out your garage. It's an important part of your home.

QUESTIONS TO ASK AN AGENT

Can you evaluate the condition of my home?

It's important to understand that you need not sign a listing with an agent in order to make this request, and get the evaluation. Agents will gladly do it for you just on the hope that you'll sign with them at some future time. And, if you like what they say, you may indeed want to. Often the agent will look at you closely to see just how serious you are, to see just how much criticism you can take. My suggestion is that you explain that you intend to sell your home, you want to find a buyer at the maximum amount of price and within the minimum amount of time, and that you realize that putting the home into great condition is one of the ways to accomplish that. Ask the agent to be brutally honest. What does he or she think of the condition of your home? Then, be prepared for the fusillade. You may discover that your home needs painting inside and out. That it needs new carpeting, a new kitchen, new lighting. If the agent begins to see your face drop, he or she may suddenly end with, "Of course, overall it looks pretty good." Don't let them off that easily. Demand to know the truth, the worst truth that you don't want to admit about your place, even if it hurts. Then evaluate the agent's evaluation. You may want to call in several agents to get different opinions. If all the opinions coincide, however, then you have learned something valuable about your home. And you can decide whether the market is so hot that it will sell in spite of its problems. Or, if in a slower market, you will likely have to cut your price to get a sale. Or you're going to have to bite the bullet and do the recommended work.

Is the house clean enough to show?

Cleanliness may be next to Godliness, but in a home for sale it's simply a necessity. Some agents will take it upon themselves, as soon as they sign up a listing, to call in a cleaning crew (which they pay for) to wash and clean-up the kitchen, bathroom(s), and other rooms. Others may simply point out to you what you need to do to get the house in shape. Don't be surprised if they mention keeping all dishes, pots, and pans clean and out of sight, washing the floors in kitchens and baths, cleaning windows, and so forth. They are simply telling you to get your house up to par for buyers, who are always highly critical. Yes, it may be clean enough for you to live in, but it needs to be spotless to convince someone to actually pay money for it.

Are there any big-ticket items I need to fix or replace?

Beyond simply cleaning, the agent may suggest, if he or she hasn't already done so, that you get new carpet, or a new stove in the kitchen, or a new sink in the bathroom. However, don't expect the agent to insist or even to push this very strongly. After all, we're quickly moving into the realm of home renovation and most agents know that money spent here is rarely returned on a dollar-for-dollar basis. The agent is most likely to be concerned with appearances. He or she wants your home to look its best and if you can get away with just cleaning the carpets, why replace them?

What about the heating/air?

Then there are the items that can't be seen, the various systems of the home. The biggest of these is the heating and air conditioning. If these are both working, the agent will almost certainly say don't bother. It won't matter if the heater isn't quite up to par in the dead of winter or the air conditioner can't keep it freezer cold in the heat of summer. The fact that you have them and that they work usually is all that matters. On the other hand, if they don't work, it's a different story. Expect the agent to insist that you get them fixed. He or she will correctly point out that the buyer almost certainly will get a professional inspection which will reveal the problem. Then the buyer will demand it be fixed, or worse, demand it be replaced. Better to fix the problem now, on your own terms, then later when you may have to act under a buyer's demands. *Note:* Sometimes these things can't be fixed. I recently had a 27-year-old heater/air conditioner go out. An inspection revealed that the heat exchanger on the heater was cracked, which could release toxic gases into the house. Now it was a health and safety issue. I could, of course, simply disclose the problem to a buyer and sell the house as is. But, I knew that would cause the price to be severely reduced. So I bit the bullet and endured the pain of paying for a new system. (It made no sense to put an old air conditioning system onto a new heater, so both were replaced.) However, now I had a selling point. I could show the buyer that the heater/air were brand new. No, it might not get much more in price for me. But, it could result in a quicker sale since the buyer wouldn't be worrying about replacing these items.

What about the plumbing?

The agent may turn on the water in several sinks to see if there's sufficient pressure. And flush the toilets to see if they operate. Assuming everything works, the story should end here. Unfortunately, however, it sometimes doesn't. Many homes built over 30 years ago had galvanized iron pipes installed. At the time, this was considered an appropriate way to handle potable water in the home. Unfortunately, over time and given sediments in the water (and sometimes electrolytic action with the soil), these pipes rust and spring leaks. The result is that suddenly a pipe can burst spreading water throughout the house. And one leak usually meant others are soon coming. I've seen some of these old pipes look like Swiss cheese because they had so many holes in them. If this is the case in your house, the agent may suggest you repipe to new copper plumbing. The cost may be $10,000 or more. On the other hand, revealing that you have leaking galvanized iron pipes, can cause many sellers to shy away from your property. (Not revealing this problem when you know about it could result in real problems *after* the sale once the buyers get their first leak.) Short-term solutions include replacing just the few pipes that are currently leaking or putting pressure seals around them (at best, a temporary fix). If your agent suggests replacing the piping in your home, give it serious consideration. In an area where this is a common problem and buyers are aware of the cost of fixing it, by doing it you might not only get a quicker sale, but much of your money back in a higher price.

What about the roof?

Probably the single most costly item to replace in a house is the roof. At minimum, the price is going to be $5000 to $10,000. Depending on the type and quality of roof the price just goes up from there. However, you can't really sell a house with a leaking roof (unless you sell "as is" and disclose the problem, which means the buyers will usually subtract the cost of the most expensive roof they can get from the price they offer). Your agent may ask you if the roof leaks. If you tell him or her it does (don't try to conceal this obvious fact), the agent may simply say, "Get it fixed!" If the roof is still fairly new, a roofer may be able to handle this for you for a nominal cost. But, if the roof is old, at or beyond its life expectancy, you may need to consider a new one. (*Note:* A worn roof doesn't just leak in one spot—it leaks all over making replacement a necessity.) Your two alternate choices (outside of putting on a new roof) are to get it fixed yourself, at the best price you can. Or to give the buyers an allowance toward getting it fixed after the sale. The problem with the latter course is that a lender may require the roof be fixed *prior* to the close of escrow. And/or the buyers may try to negotiate a more costly roof than is currently on the house, for more money than you want to spend.

Is the carpet in good enough condition to sell the house?

The carpet doesn't necessarily have to be new. But it must be clean (no spots or dirt) and it shouldn't look worn. In many cases, you can clean a dirty carpet and it will come out looking fine, but not always. Some spots are permanent. Ask the agent for advice, here. There's very little you can do to make a worn carpet look better. Therefore, you may want to bite the bullet and replace the carpeting. Even inexpensive new carpeting will usually look far better than dirty or worn old carpeting, at least for the first 6 months to a year. *Warning:* Beware of pet odors, particularly urine, in the carpeting. These are almost impossible to remove and usually mandate replacement of carpet and padding.

Is there anything detracting about the house that you see?

This is a catch-all question. When you've finally finished fixing up your home, go back and take a second, and perhaps even a third look. Call in a friend, neighbor, and/or agent to look with you. What have you overlooked? Maybe there's a big, ugly chandelier in the dining room that catches everyone's attention, and not in a favorable way. Or perhaps the scratches on a countertop are what draw interest away from the rest of the kitchen. Find the big detractor, if there is one, and work on it to complete the presentation of your home.

2
How to Find a Good Agent

QUESTIONS TO ASK YOURSELF

Have I tried selling my house "by owner"?

□

Before asking an agent to sell your home for you, I believe every seller should consider doing it by him- or herself. The obvious reason is that you could save a lot of money on commissions. The not so obvious reason is that if you gave some of that saved money to a buyer, you might get a quicker sale. However, having asked the question, it's important to understand that selling on your own takes time, effort, and experience (and a little seed money). If you have none of these, then don't proceed any farther along this line. Just start looking for a good agent (see below). On the other hand, if you think you might be able to sell "by owner," then go immediately to Chapter 9, which details how to do it and explains the rewards and perils involved. (By the way, only about 10 percent of sellers actually succeed in selling homes on their own without an agent.)

Do I have a recommendation for a good agent?

□

A recommendation can go a long way. Perhaps a relative, friend, or even associate recently sold their home and had a good experience. They were pleased with the work their agent did for them and can wholeheartedly recommend him or her. Get the name and phone number of this agent and call them up and interview them (see below). A good recommendation is like gold. It can lead to greater wealth. A word of caution, however. Sometimes people only think they've had good service. Perhaps they were entranced by the agent's smooth style. Or maybe the house sold itself the first day on the market. Possibly they only think they got a good deal, when in reality they ended up getting far less than the home is worth. Or, in a worst case scenario, perhaps the agent offered to give them a hundred bucks for each recommendation they made to friends who eventually listed with the agent. All of which is to say, take every recommendation with a grain of salt.

Have I looked for *local* real estate offices?

It's important to understand that regardless of how big a national real estate company may be, it all comes down to neighborhoods. Real estate is sold one house at a time, and buyers go out to local areas to search for the homes they want. Consider: If you were a buyer who wanted to purchase a home in a Minitonka, Minnesota neighborhood, where would you most likely go to find a real estate agent? Would you go to an office near the neighborhood? Or would you go to an office across town? In a different town? In a different state? While a buyer might choose any of those, or might go with an agent who he or she knew, chances are they'd first try a neighborhood office. After all, the agents in a local office should know the area best. That's why you want to have your property listed with one of those *local* agents. You greatly improve your chances of getting a quicker sale for more money *if* you list with a real estate company physically close to your home.

Have I gone to "open houses" in my area?

Being a seller, you may find this a strange question. Why check into open houses that are being offered by other sellers? There are two very good reasons: One is to check out the competition. The other, to find a real estate agent by seeing him or her in action. Agents don't hold an open house so much to sell the particular home they are in. (They know that buyers rarely purchase a home as a result of attending an open house.) Rather, agents are looking for buyers and sellers with whom they can work. Thus, when you walk into an open house, the very first question an agent is likely to ask you, after of course your

name, is if you've already sold your home. If not, then
you become a prime candidate for a client. This agent
would just love to sign you to a listing. But before doing
that, watch how the agent works. How does he or she
deal with other people who come by the open house? Do
you like the agent's manner? Are you impressed with the
agent's knowledge? Does the agent's forthrightness and
honesty feel right? If so, then invite the agent to see your
house. And interview him or her as noted below.

Have I narrowed the field to one particular agent?

You don't want to list with many agents. You want to list
with one agent who will give you great service. Some sellers have heard of "open" listings. Here, you list your
property with all agents who come by. You promise to
pay a commission to the lucky one who finds you a buyer.
It's one of those traps that sounds oh so good, but in reality is oh so bad. The reason is that by listing with all
agents, you give no one an incentive to work hard on selling your property. *Consider:* Why should any one agent
work hard when any other might suddenly pop up with
a buyer to claim the full commission? The better way is to
list exclusively with one agent. That agent can then co-
broke with all the other agents in the area, which is what's
commonly done. Your agent puts your listing on the MLS
(Multiple Listing Service) or some other interagency listing service and all the agents in the area cooperate. But no
matter who sells the property, your agent gets a cut of the
commission. And because he or she is assured of this,
your agent works very, very hard (hopefully) to find you
a good buyer. It's a case where doing something that's
counterintuitive is actually the right answer.

Have I interviewed that agent?

Recommendations are great. Having an office in your
neighborhood is a plus. Seeing the agent in action at an
open house is an even bigger plus. But, before signing
a listing agreement, you should sit down and conduct a
thorough interview. Think of it as hiring an employee.
While the agent isn't exactly an employee (more of a free-
lancer), you want to do the kind of interviewing you
might do for anyone who'll work for you. After all, you're

going to be paying a hefty commission to the agent, so you should be sure you're getting your money's worth. In the section below we'll discuss the questions to ask your agent. However, a word to those who feel awkward about conducting an interview. In short, don't worry about it. A good agent will expect to be interviewed and will have ready answers to all your questions. A poor agent may be put out by your questions and even become indignant. Don't worry about it. You wouldn't want that person to represent you, anyway. Do an interview. You'll learn a lot. You'll get the information you need to make a big financial decision—selecting your own personal real estate agent.

Did I get pressured by the agent?

A big part of an agent's job, after all, is selling. And selling can involve actively working to get a buyer to make an acceptable offer on your home. You want an assertive agent. You don't want an agent who's a wimp, who simply lets buyers off the hook. On the other hand, what's good for the goose can sometimes be bad for the gander. While you want the agent to be assertive with buyers, you don't necessarily want him or her to be assertive with you. While you may want the agent to pressure a buyer into making an offer, you don't want that agent to pressure you into accepting an offer. You want an agent who will offer advice and explanations, not one who tries to shove an offer down your throat. But finding an agent who is both a assertive for buyers, yet a thoughtful advisor for sellers is not an easy thing to do. Therefore, my suggestion is that you over- look a little bit of pressure that an agent may apply to get you to list. It goes with the territory. It's part of being a good salesperson. On the other hand, I also suggest that you avoid agents who are strictly high-pressure operators. You'll know one when you run across one. They'll be wav- ing that listing agreement in your face. They'll be telling you how terrific a salesperson they are. How lousy other agents are. (I never deal with anyone who runs down a competitor.) What a big opportunity this is for you to sign with them. How lucky that they have time to deal with you. And on and on. I hope you get the picture. Avoid an agent who pressures you to list. Because if you don't, you will probably get that same pressure, or more, to sign a sales agreement that just might not be favorable to you.

Does the agent seem knowledgeable?

Do you know anything about real estate? Most people know at least something. Perhaps you've sold a house in the past, or bought one. Maybe you have some experience as a renter. Try to think of an experience you had in the past in which you know the outcome. Then ask the agent about it. Does the agent seem to know at least as much as you do? In order to get a real estate license (agents are licensed in all 50 states), an agent must pass a fairly rigorous exam. However, having passed that exam does not guarantee that an agent knows a lot about the business. It just means the agent knew the answers to most of the questions asked on the test. You, however, want an agent who, hopefully, has vast knowledge of the entire field. You need a knowledgeable agent to lead you past the minefield of legal and practical problems that can occur when you sell your home.

Is the agent experienced?

Experience counts. Would you want to be a passenger on an airliner where the pilot was making his or her first run? What about the patient of a surgeon doing his or her first appendectomy? Or, the client of an attorney trying his or her first case? Yes, someone has to be first. But, if at all possible, try to be sure it's not you! You want the benefit of an agent's vast experience. That way, if something is wrong with the deal, the agent will recognize it in time to make corrections. Or, if something goes very badly, the agent will know how to save your lunch. Check the questions to ask below that pertain to experience and be sure that the agent's answer reveals someone who has spent many, many years learning the business.

Does the agent know all about homes in my area?

This is easy. You know all about the homes in your neighborhood, right? After all, you live there. You certainly know about your home. And chances are you've visited with other neighbors. You know floorplans, layouts, yards, and streets. You know parks and recreational facilities. You know about schools, shopping, and even if there's a problem with criminal activity. In short, if you've lived in your home for more than a few months, you should be an expert in your area. But, if your agent is on top of the area he or she "farms" (a *farm* is an area that an agent prospects for listings), he or she should also know a lot about many neighborhood topics. Thus, after talking with the agent for awhile, you should begin to get an impression of his or her knowledge of homes in your area. Does the agent know the floorplans? (A good agent will even know the names of different floorplans as given by the builder—something you may not know.) Does the agent know about schools and parks? (He or she should be able to tell you the percentile test scores of your schools or whether or not a new park is in development, again something you may not know.) In other words, not only should a good agent know most of what you know about your neighborhood, he or she should know even more about it than you.

Does the agent seem honest?

How does one really know if another person is honest? It's one of the hardest things to determine. However, over the years I've learned to trust my sixth sense about this sort of thing. Just in case you haven't yet had a chance to develop your sixth sense, here are some things I look out for. I listen carefully to everything the agent says. If the agent begins slamming other agents, or others in the field, telling me how bad they are, I sense a problem. At the least this agent is not professional. At the worst, he or she is telling tales out of school, many of which may be fabricated. If the agent begins telling me how he or she tricked a buyer into giving a seller a better deal (hoping to impress me with how well he or she takes care of seller clients), I get worried. In real estate, as in all else, the best deals are where everyone wins. If the agent "tricked" a buyer, how do I know this agent won't try to "trick" me in the future? If the agent exaggerates by telling me I can get a higher price than I know is realistic or a quicker deal than seems possible, I get turned off. This agent may not be outright lying, but exaggeration is close to it. If the agent is building an unrealistic world of expectations in me, it can only result in problems down the road. Most of all I listen to see if what the agent tells me sounds sensible. Remember, all it takes to unravel a dishonest person is one small lie.

Can the agent give me references?

I may have found this agent because of a personal referral
from a relative, friend, or neighbor. But once found, I
would expect the agent to be able to provide me with a
list of satisfied clients. If the agent earlier tells me he or
she has sold 15 houses over the past year or two, then this
agent should be able to provide me with a list of 15 satisfied clients whom I can call to verify the good job that was
done. A good agent will be delighted to provide you with
references. After all, your asking means you're seriously
considering listing with this person and good references
should just cement the deal. On the other hand, if the
agent stumbles and says he or she will need to put
together a list and get back to me, I start to get worried. If
the agent never does produce a list... or if that list is
short... or if it doesn't have phone numbers, I look for
another agent. An additional word of caution: Just
because you get a long list of names and phone numbers,
doesn't mean those people on the list are real. They could
be relatives, friends doing a favor, or even clients who
really didn't have a good experience. All of which is to
say, when your prospective agent gives you a list of references, *call them*! Too many sellers simply believe that
because an agent is bold enough to produce a reference
list, it must be proof positive of the agent's quality.
Baloney, check out everything!

Would I be willing to trust this agent with my personal finances?

Some people tend to think of real estate agents as less professional than other financial advisors. For example, you
might trust your most sensitive financial dealings (checking and savings account locations and balances, invest-
ments, alimony, etc.) to your attorney, your accountant, or
your financial planner. After all, these are the professionals who you rely on to give you the advice needed to protect yourself financially. On the other hand, would you
give this same information to your real estate agent? Why
not? After all, your agent is involved in what for most people is the largest financial transaction they will make in
their entire lifetime—selling their home. I'm not suggesting that you need to give your real estate agent sensitive

financial information. Most of the time you don't. What I'm suggesting is that you pick someone to be your agent with whom you would feel perfectly comfortable sharing this information. Your agent needs to be a professional, like the others. If you don't feel your agent is a professional, then find one who is.

Have I called the Better Business Bureau?

Few people ever do. Yet, real estate companies belong to the Better Business Bureau (BBB) just as do many merchants. And the BBB will be happy to tell you if they've received no complaints about the agent or the company, or if they have complaints as long as their arm. But, you may be saying, nobody does this sort of thing. Think again—careful people do. After all, what can you lose? It's only a phone call. Your agent will probably never know that you made it. And when you learn that the agent you're considering has a perfect record, think how much better you'll feel! On the other hand, if you learn your agent has a long list of complaints, you'll thank yourself for discovering this *before* you listed, not after. Of course, keep in mind that just because the BBB has no complaints doesn't prove your agent is spotless. Many people don't complain even after they've been injured.

Have I checked with my state's department of real estate?

All states have a real estate department, although it may go under a variety of names. (In California, for example, it's called "The Division of Real Estate.") One of the primary purposes of this department is to police real estate agents. When a complaint is filed against an agent, normally the department will investigate. The degree and speed of the investigation usually correlates directly with how many complaints are received. When the department finds a serious problem, it often will call a hearing after which it may suspend or revoke the agent's license. It also will sometimes allow the agent to continue in business with a restricted license, one limited to only certain kinds of transactions. However, you won't know if any of this has happened to your agent, unless you call your department of real estate. The call is usually quite simple to make. You simply find out where the department is located (typically in the state capital and part of the business and finance department). Sometimes these departments can be most easily reached by email. Other times, a phone call is quicker. Just give the agent's full name (which you should already know) and the address. You should quickly find out if any problems are current, and in some cases, if there were problems in the past. Keep in mind, however, that these investigations are normally done only for serious violations of the law, usually involving stolen or mismanaged funds. Rarely will a department of real estate investigate because a buyer or seller was unhappy with the general performance of an agent, as long as no laws were broken.

Have I called trade organizations?

Trade organizations are a good source of information, although they tend to feel a responsibility to protect their members, so sometimes they are less forthcoming with information. However, at the least they can sometimes inform you if an agent is an active member and what advanced degrees he or she holds. The largest of these organizations is the National Association of REALTORS® (NAR), and it offers many such degrees obtained by passing rigorous classes. These include Certified Residential Specialist (CRS), Graduate of the REALTOR Institute (GRI), General Accredited Appraiser (GAA), and many others. You can reach the NAR online at *www.realtor.org*. Their phone number in Chicago is 800-874-6500.

QUESTIONS TO ASK AN AGENT

Are you a licensed agent?

Every state requires anyone who offers to sell real estate for a commission, in other words an agent, to be licensed. While licensing requirements vary somewhat, in most cases they involve passing both a rigorous exam and serving an apprenticeship under an experienced broker, usually for 2 years. This doesn't mean, however, that everyone who offers to "list" your home is licensed. Sometimes, for example, a neighbor may offer to sell your house for you. This usually occurs when you're living elsewhere and your home is rented or vacant. The neighbor may say, "Let me try selling your place. If I'm successful, you can pay me $5000. If I'm not, you haven't lost anything." Since this amount is probably less than a broker's commission, you may be tempted. But beware. While there's nothing wrong with having a neighbor watch over your property while you're away, there can be all sorts of problems if that neighbor doesn't have a license and attempts to sell it for you. Your neighbor might get an offer from a buyer and write it up incorrectly, embroiling you in all sorts of legal entanglements. Your neighbor may make commitments in your name, which you might not want to honor. On the other hand, your neighbor couldn't enforce a claim for the commission without a license. All of which is to say, don't take chances. Be sure the person you're dealing with is a licensed agent. If you're not sure, simply ask to see their license or call your state's real estate licensing department.

Are you a salesperson or a broker?

In real estate there are two classes of agents. A "full" agent, or one who can open an office, complete deals, and collect commissions is called a broker. Most people assume that all agents they talk with are brokers. This is not usually the case. Most agents are actually salespeople. A salesperson is a limited agent, restricted by the fact that he or she cannot independently open an office nor collect a commission. Rather, the salesperson must work under the direct supervision and auspices of a broker. This is not to say that a broker is necessarily more experienced, wiser, or better to deal with than a salesperson. Indeed, many very good brokers will opt to put their license *under* another broker and work as a salesperson. Why? Because they don't want the management responsibilities, the liability, and the cost of operating an office. Besides, in today's market, a really good agent (broker or salesperson) can often command as much as 80 percent of the commission that goes to the broker's office. (The usual split is 50-50.) The broker is willing to pay such a high split because the agent (broker or salesperson) is such a good "producer," bringing in many sales. You should ask, however, if your agent is a broker or salesperson. If they answer a broker working as a salesperson under another

broker, ask what their commission split is. Most will tell
you. A very high split usually indicates a very experienced agent. On the other hand, a 50-50 split may indicate
a broker who simply can't make it in the business on his
or her own and is just hanging on in this office; perhaps
someone who might not be your wisest choice. If the
agent says he or she is a salesperson, you can ask if they
are going through their apprenticeship. If so, again you
may want to opt for a more experienced agent.

How many years of experience do you have?

As with most fields, the more experience the better. A real
estate agent who has been around for 20 years actively
pursuing the business has probably run into every sort of
transaction, complication, and pitfall that can occur. And
if some new problem should pop up, chances are this
agent will have a bag of tricks ready to deal with it. In
short, you can benefit from the agent's experience in
order to get a quicker sale and one that avoids complica-
tions. On the other hand, if the agent answers that he or
she has only been in the business a short time, then you're
probably more at risk. Most learning in real estate does
not come out of books. It comes from the "school of hard
knocks." And, quite frankly, a newer agent may simply
not have knocked around enough to be able to give you
great service. Of course, this is not to say that everyone
should avoid novice agents. If they did, how would any
agent ever get any experience?! On the other hand, you
have to ask yourself the question, "Do I want my agent to
learn on me?" I would consider 5 years in the business to
be minimum.

How many homes did you list last year?

If you were going to have surgery, would you want a
doctor who had performed half a dozen similar procedures in the past? Or one who had performed thousands of them? If it were me, I'd want the doctor who
knew the surgery backward and forward from having
done it so many times. All of which is to say that while
being in the business a long time is a good indicator, it
is not the only sign you should look for. After all, this
agent could be one who has sat on his or her backside

for 20 years and seldom listed or sold a home. (He or she probably has an outside income, as we'll discuss shortly.) You want an *active* agent, one who is constantly listing properties. If the agent answers that he or she listed three homes last year, be wary. If they listed six, you can be comfortable. If they listed nine, chances are you're still doing okay. On the other hand, if they answer they listed 20, watch out. You could be in the hands of a "lister only." This is an agent who firmly believes the old adage, "Those who list, last." Some agents make it their entire work to simply list homes, put them on the MLS for other agents to sell, and then go out and list other properties. They provide little to no servicing of their clients. If the listed house sells, they collect the commission. If it doesn't, they're on to other sellers. Beware of an agent who's listed more than 12 properties in a year. Generally speaking, it's very hard for an agent to properly service six listings. Assuming one sells every two months, that's a year's worth. In a hot market, perhaps one a month may sell. But more than that and you might not get the service you want, need, and deserve.

Of those, how many sold?

What's a good batting average? Is it 50 percent? 60 percent? I've known agents whose batting average, year in and year out, is close to 90 to 100 percent. If they list a property, it's as good as sold. Isn't this the kind of agent you want? Of course, you also must determine the "why" of such a high percentage of sales. Is it because the agent helped price the properties right, saw they were fixed up for showing, determinedly publicized them, showed the homes, and otherwise did everything in his or her power to make the sales? Or is it because this agent browbeat sellers into asking such low prices that the homes were sure to sell because buyers saw them as "bargain basement values"? You want the diligent agent first mentioned, not the high-pressure variety. If you get the latter, you'll quickly realize it as they typically spend a lot of time running down your property and trying to get you to price it far below what you probably think it's worth. (See also Chapter 3 on accurate pricing.)

Do you have other sources of income?   □

Is this question too personal to ask your agent? I don't
think so, not when you'll be entrusting the sale of what's
probably your largest asset to him or her. What you're
really asking is whether or not the agent will spend full
time working on the sale of your property. Or, if the agent
has other income, whether selling real estate is just a part-
time job in which he or she devotes part-time efforts. A
great many people in real estate are actually retirees. They
are retired from the military, teaching, large corporations,
and elsewhere. They have retirement income, usually
enough on which to get by. And they've gotten into real
estate to help with the extras. If they sell a property, it's
great for them. On the other hand, if they don't, well then,
they still can get by. The biggest problem with the part-
timer, however, is that he or she simply isn't hungry
enough. They might be a seal lazily sunning on a rock
waiting for a big fish to come by, instead of a shark constantly on the prowl for food. You want the shark on your
side. Therefore, asking if the agent has outside income is
not an unreasonable question. Of course, sometimes
agents will have related income, such as property management— handling the rental of homes for others.
There's nothing wrong with this, as long as it doesn't take
up so much of the agent's time that there's nothing left for
selling (as can many times happen with property management). In general, look for agents who are fully committed to real estate. If they don't sell, they don't get by.

How did you present the offers on those that sold?   □

This is an interesting and important question. After all,
hopefully soon this agent will be coming to you with an
offer. Did the agent present every offer as it came in? Or
did he or she wait until sellers made a decision on one
offer before presenting the next? (Legally and ethically
agents are required to present all offers as they come in so
you have the greatest opportunity to accept the best.)
Were the offers presented by the buyer's agent with your
agent present? (In a very hot market, buyers' agents often
just FAX an offer in and it's then up to the listing agent to
explain it.) Was every attempt made to reach the seller as

soon as there was an offer, or if out of town, did the agent wait until the seller got back? (Many agents will wait— not a good idea as the buyer may get other ideas in the interim and pull the offer.) Finally, does the agent speak of convincing unsure sellers to take the plunge and sign, of hand-holding, of getting sellers to be "man enough" to do it, and so on, all of which suggest undue pressure tactics? Remember, you want a helpful agent, not a high-pressure salesperson.

Do you suggest any special "tips" to get better bids?

In the superheated market of the last few years, agents have come up with a variety of "tips" to help sellers get more for their homes. Sometimes these work. Sometimes they don't. One that has received lots of play in the hottest markets is called "buyer's frenzy." Here the agent tells the sellers to leave town for a week or two right after they list. Thus, when buyers begin making offers, the sellers aren't around to see or accept/decline them. As more buyers see the property, and realize that other buyers are making offers on it, they sometimes start to bid higher. A bidding frenzy ensues and by the time the sellers return, often there are offers for *more* than the asking price on the property! When this works, the sellers are thrilled. On the other hand, the great danger is that there might only be one or two offers and by the sellers not being available, the buyers may withdraw the offers leaving the house unsold. Thus, this ploy could backfire. Other tricks involve "underpricing" and "range-pricing." (See Chapter 3 on pricing for further details.) All of these offer advantages and have down sides. While the agent's ethics in using these tricks is questionable, what's important to you is whether you fully understand both the advantages they might offer, as well as the dangers they pose.

On how many sales did you represent both the seller and the buyer?

What you are really asking here is if your agent found the buyer for the homes he or she listed. This is important because, as noted earlier, you want to avoid a "lister only." You want an active agent who's out there not only listing properties, but also finding buyers for them as well. This usually helps ensure a quicker sale for you. And there's an additional plus. When a single agent finds both buyer and seller, there's an added incentive to make the deal work. After all, the agent is not just getting the selling agent's half of the commission (typically 3 percent of a total 6 percent commission), but the entire commission, the full 5, 6, 7, or whatever percent was agreed on in the listing. While it won't happen every time, in these circumstances, if both buyer and seller cannot come to terms in the negotiations and can't close the deal, occasionally the agent may throw in a part of his or her commission to make it all happen. Because the agent is getting a full commission, he or she has more to play with... more to throw in to make the deal go through..

Do you work on weekends as well as during the week?

I simply can't conceive of an agent not working on the weekends. After all, that's when buyers have time to go out and look at property. However, my son recently moved to a town in Connecticut and when I told him to call agents on the weekend in order to see homes, he reported that of the seven he called, all seven had their offices closed—they didn't work on weekends! To my way of thinking, either these agents were such fat cats that they simply didn't need the business, or they just didn't know that buyers were out there on the weekends, or the custom in the area was for everything to close on Saturday and Sunday. I must say, however, that this is the exception. In most areas of the country, the weekend is the busiest time for agents. If your agent says he or she works hard during the week and takes time off to rest on the weekend, my suggestion is that you find a different agent. You want that workaholic who's out there pounding the pavements 7 days a week for you.

How often do you plan on calling to tell me how things are going?

Again, an important question. You want to be kept informed. Besides, you may have useful suggestions to make. Agents will often answer truthfully; after all they don't want to set up an unrealistic anticipation in you. If they plan on calling weekly, they'll say so. And if they plan on calling only when there's news, they'll tell you that, too. And if they plan never to call, expect them to say something like, "Oh, I'll call once in awhile." Ideally, you want an agent who checks in at least once a week. For active agents, this is no hardship. After all, they're working hard to drum up business for your home (usually by telling other agents what a great deal it is—the most useful kind of work they can do), and they're happy to share their experiences with you. And, as noted, you may be able to come up with ideas to help sell the property. And if nothing else works, then between you and the agent, you may decide to do additional fix-up work, or advertising, or (shudder!) lower your price.

What kind of promotion will you do on my property?

Before listening to the answer your prospective agent may give, it's important to understand what kind of promotion will best serve your interests. For that you have to understand real estate. Houses aren't sold in a vacuum. Rather, there's a giant fraternity out there to which agents, buyers, and sellers all belong. It operates like this. Buyers want homes. To find them, nearly 90 percent first turn to agents. After all, agents are the people who have homes listed. Sellers want to sell homes and, similarly, they turn to agents because they know that's where the buyers are. Consequently, the way the game is played is that agents put buyers in touch with sellers. Just playing the odds, get enough buyers to see your home and at least one of them will want to buy it. The key is getting all those agents who have buyers focused on your house. After all, the agents can show buyers any of hundreds, perhaps thousands, of other homes in your area. You want them to show yours. For this to happen, your agent must promote your home to other agents. Remember, the chances of any one agent, including yours, finding just the right buyer for your house is remote. But, the chance of all of the agents finding just the right buyer is excellent, as long as they know about your home. Therefore, when you ask your agent about promotion, listen to hear if he or she talks about promoting it to other agents—that's the way to a sale.

Will you put my property on the Multiple Listing Service?

The best way for your agent to get other agents, one or more of whom may have just the right buyer, to work on your house is to share the listing on the Multiple Listing Service (MLS). This allows all the other MLS brokers in the area (which usually includes nearly all of them) to co-broke or share the listing. Beware of any agent who speaks of holding your home off the MLS, in other words keeping it for him- or herself, otherwise known as "vest pocketing" the listing. The agent may tell you this will result in a quicker sale or a higher price. Not likely. It usually just means that the agent wants to get the full commission instead of sharing, which usually does not benefit you.

How else will you spread the word about my house?

There are all sorts of methods agents can use to spread the word about your house to other agents. These include:

- Holding a "caravan" where agents come by over the course of a day or two to see your home.
- Holding an *agents'* open house. This is different from the conventional open house in that only agents are invited. Typically, your agent will induce other agents to come by offering some food and drink.
- Sending emails to other agents both in your agent's office and in other offices.
- Phoning other agents, both in your agent's office and in other offices.
- Standing up at meetings, which agents typically hold monthly or bi-weekly, and "talking up" your home.

What kind of "open house" will you hold?

As noted, a traditional open house aimed at the general public will likely do you little good. Most buyers rarely purchase the home they visit at an open house. (Agents know they are most likely to attract clients, buyers for other properties as well as sellers, when they hold an open house... which doesn't really help you.) On the other hand, a broker's open house is a terrific idea. To encourage your agent you may even want to help prepare some snacks (usually pastry and small sandwiches) and offer some drinks (wine as well as soft drinks). There's an old understanding in real estate that goes something like, "If you feed them, they will come!" And, of course, in the process they will see your home. Remember, the more agents who actually see your home, the better your chances are that one of them will have just the right buyer and will bring him or her by.

What kind of advertising will you do?

A plan of advertising is always part of selling any home. However, it's important to understand that just as with open houses, buyers rarely purchase the home which they call about from an ad. However, advertising does produce buyers and even if they call on another house, one of them may ultimately be interested in your property. Therefore, you want an agent whose company advertises, hopefully heavily. However, don't get into the trap of demanding that it be your house that be advertised. It's usually enough that the agent advertise homes in your price range. Don't worry, if someone calls up who's interested in a home just like yours, the agent will bring them to see your house. Additionally, other agents read advertising and since they know they can almost always co-broke a home, they may be encouraged to call your agent about a house for which they have a buyer, which could be yours.

How soon will you place a sign on my property?

It may seem obvious, but one of the best ways to find a buyer is to simply put a sign out in front. When (and if) you try to sell by owner, this will be your best selling tool. It's the same for an agent. A sign out front lets your neighbors (who may know buyers) become aware your home is for sale. It acts as a beacon to buyers who may just be riding through your neighborhood. And it helps would-be buyers who might have already called to find your property. You want your agent to put out that sign as soon as possible, on the very day your house is listed!

Will you create flyers about my house?

This is a great device to help entice buyers to learn more about your property. If you've looked at houses for sale at all, you've certainly seen them. Typically they are on a lit-tle plastic box attached to the For Sale sign. The flyer usu-ally has a photo of the home (sometimes including inside and view shots), the price, and some important features (such as the number of bedrooms and bathrooms, square footage, and specials including things like fireplaces, spas, extra rooms, and so on). And, of course, it includes contact information about the agent. The better flyers are done in color, since this shows off the picture(s) better. These flyers also can be distributed elsewhere, such as at agents' meetings. For you, the important thing is that the agent create a flyer and get it out there. Many agents will say they will keep the box on the For Sale sign filled. I don't believe it. Agents have so many things to do that running out to your house before every weekend (when buyers are most likely to come by) and fill up a box of fly-ers is just not going to happen. Better if the agent sug-gests, or you offer, to keep the box filled from a supply the agent gives you. After all, if you're living in the home, how hard is it to occasionally go out there and refill the box of flyers?

Will you act as a seller's agent, buyer's agent, or dual agent?

This is important for you to know as it helps define how much you can rely on the agent's advice. Remember, it doesn't make any difference who pays the agent. It's up to the agent to declare for whom he or she works. While most likely the agent will say he or she works for you, don't take it for granted. Although highly unlikely, the agent could declare he or she works for the buyer. If an agent works for the buyer, then take whatever he or she says with a big grain of salt – remember, they're trying to get the best deal they can for that buyer, not you. More likely, if the agent finds a buyer for your home, he or she could declare as a "dual agent," or one representing both parties. I don't know if you've ever tried working for two bosses simultaneously, but that's what it's like for an agent to represent both buyer and seller—in reality an almost impossible task. Therefore, if I'm listing with an agent and paying a commission to that agent (although, as I said, this technically doesn't matter), I'm going to demand that the agent be strictly a seller's agent. Later, when that agent comes to me and says, "I've found a buyer and I'm going to represent both of you as a dual agent," I'll have a big decision to make. I can say, nope, you're representing me only. This will make the agent cringe because it could mean losing a full commission and having to settle for half. Or, if I see some advantage to me (such as a cut in the commission), I may agree. Sometimes I'll do it if I truly respect the agent and believe he or she will be able to represent both my interests and those of the buyer.

Will you handle all the paperwork?

You'd think this would go without saying. But not necessarily. I've never heard of a full-service broker, one to whom you're paying a full commission, refusing to do the paperwork. On the other hand, if you're using a discount broker (paying less than a full commission), it's a possibility. It won't hurt to ask. And if the agent says he or she isn't doing all the paperwork, find out what part of it is being left to you. After all, it might mean that you'd need to hire the services of an attorney to get the deal finished, or at least get instructions on handling it from the agent. (Usually the agent will handle the purchase agreement by which the deal is made. But other paperwork, such as disclosures, escrow instructions, termite clearances, and so on might just be left up to you.)

What professional organizations do you belong to?

It's not necessary for an agent to belong to any trade organization to sell real estate. Just possessing a license is enough. But trade organizations provide information, education, legal and technical help, and much more. In fact, they provide so many benefits to an agent that I can't imagine one not belonging. So if your agent doesn't belong, be sure to ask why. Could it be that the agent was thrown out? If so, that's usually done only for bad conduct, which should be a telling blow to your desires to list with him or her. The vast majority of agents belong to the National Association of REALTORS® (NAR). There are various categories of membership offered to both brokers and agents. If your agent is a member, he or she will proudly tell you so. Also ask if they have any advanced degrees offered through the NAR. (See "Have I called trade organizations?" above.)

Has a state real estate department ever taken action against you? □

This is a tough question to ask someone with whom you are planning to work, since it implies mistrust. However, it's important to find out. If your prospective agent has had his or her license suspended or revoked at some time in the past, even though it's currently active, knowing about it could very well influence your decision to list. Sometimes you can couch this question in an explanation such as, "Please don't be offended and don't take this personally, but I'm interviewing many agents and as a matter of course, I'm asking each of them about this." That should do it; however, if you still feel awkward, blame it on me. Say you were reading a book on selling your home by Robert Irwin and the author suggested you ask this question. Remember, there are no foolish questions except those that aren't asked.

Are you the focus of any real estate lawsuits? □

As above, it's an awkward question. However, I'm reminded of a roofer I called a few years ago to fix a rental property I had. The roofer seemed honest and straightforward, so I hired him. However, half way through roofing my property, he quit and was gone for 5 months (before he eventually came back to finish the job). It turned out he was being sued by another property owner for doing a bad job and, as a result of that suit, he temporarily lost his contractor's license (hence, the hiatus). Something like this conceivably could happen to your agent if he or she is involved in a real estate lawsuit. Therefore, the question isn't unreasonable. And if there should be a lawsuit (even though the overall real estate agency might not be involved and your listing not directly affected), wouldn't you like to know about it and why some client brought it?

3
Pricing to Market

QUESTIONS TO ASK YOURSELF

Do I have a price in mind?

Most of us think we know what our house is worth. Since the big run-up in real estate prices at the turn of the century, most homeowners have carefully watched sales prices soar in their neighborhoods. Now, when it's time to sell, understandably we want more. We want our share of the real estate boom. And we should get it. However, it's important to understand that the market not only goes up, but sometimes it also goes down, and sometimes even sideways. Therefore, determining the right price right now has to be more scientific than guesswork. If you think you know what your home is worth, keep that price in mind. But then investigate to find out how realistic it really is.

Have I received a comparative market analysis from an agent?

A comparative market analysis (CMA) gathers together information on all the recent home sales in your neighborhood and then compares each of those to your home. It works on the theory that if a home just like yours sold for X amount of dollars, then yours ought to be worth a similar amount. A good CMA will have half a dozen homes in it that sold within the last 6 months to a year. It compares square footage, number of bedrooms and bathrooms, location, and amenities of those homes with your house. It increases for features your house has that the selling house didn't have, and decreases when it goes the other way. Ultimately, it arrives at a price estimate based on the previous sales. Almost any real estate agent will be happy to prepare a written CMA for you in the hopes of eventually getting your listing. All you have to do is ask.

41

Can I rely on the CMA?

Yes… and no. You can rely on the CMA to tell you what a home like yours sold for in the past. But, things may have changed since those earlier homes sold. Interest rates may have gone up or down. The economy in your area may be better or worse. Demand may be stronger or weaker. Thus, you have to adjust your CMA accordingly. Complicating the matter is the fact that sometimes there haven't been recent sales in your area, so you have no means of comparison. Or the homes that sold really weren't comparable to yours. Thus, you should not only ask an agent for his or her input as to your home's current value, but you should analyze the market yourself.

Have I checked out comparable homes?

The one best way to evaluate a comparable sale is to check out the house. At the least, you can drive by. From the outside you can assess the condition of the front yard, the presentation of the house itself (paint, windows, doors, and so on), and the driveway and walkup. Is the house the same plan as yours? Is it in as good a condition? Better? Sometimes it's even possible to do more. You may simply go up to the front door and knock. Introduce yourself. Explain that you live down the street and are putting your house up for sale. You're trying to determine what price to ask and understand this home recently sold. Are these people the buyers? Can they help you with pricing? I've found people to be friendly and generous with their time and assistance. Chances are you'll be invited in and can get a good look at the home. (Of course, there are security issues and in some neighborhoods, you won't want to do this.) Is it the same floorplan as yours? Is it as well decorated? Better? By assessing and comparing the similar home, you can get a clearer idea of current value for your home.

Have I become a pretend buyer for a weekend?

Another way to determine the market value of your home is to size up the competition. Chances are that at any given time there are several homes similar to yours for sale in your neighborhood. Any real estate agent should be able to tell you about these. You should be able to discover most of them by just driving down nearby streets and looking for For Sale signs. If you know a friendly agent, he or she can usually arrange for you to visit these homes so you can see firsthand what other sellers in your price range are offering. (Most agents are happy to do this in the hopes of getting your listing.) Very quickly you'll see how much worse, or better, these properties are. And you might get some good ideas about fixing up your home so it shows better. Keep in mind, however, that *asking prices* are not usually *selling prices*. Depending on the market, most homes sell for less (or sometimes more!) than the asking price.

Have I determined the price spread?

The price spread is the difference between asking price and selling price for most homes. Again, an agent can provide you this information by giving you a list of homes that shows both their asking and their selling price. You can total both figures and then get the percentage difference. In an average market, homes typically sell for around 5 percent less than asking price. In a bad market, that figure can drop to below 10 percent. Of course, in a hot market, most may sell right at asking price, or even higher! Use this information when pricing your home. Keep in mind, however, that you can't arbitrarily set a price you want and then boost it by 5 percent (or whatever), *unless* your asking price remains competitive. You have to start with the competitive asking price and then work backward to what you'll net out. (When calculating your net, don't forget transaction costs including commission, escrow, and title insurance.)

Have I taken into account recent price increases?

Here's an interesting method of calculating value. You now should be able to come up with three figures:

- **CMA:** From your CMA you should be able to determine what recent comparables *sold* for, thus giving you a price basis.

- **Current pricing:** From evaluating current homes on the market you should have a sense of what current homesellers are asking – current *asking prices*.

- **Spread:** And by comparing previous asking prices to current asking prices, you should have a good idea of the spread.

Thus, assuming the spread stays the same, you can determine if values have gone up or down. It's easy. Say you know the average spread between asking price and final sales price is 5 percent. And your competitors are pricing their homes today at an average of $200,000. You know that they should expect to receive around $190,000 as the sale price (asking price less spread equals sales price). However, by checking the CMA you also know that the average sales price during the past year was $180,000. Thus, you've learned that values in your neighborhood have gone up by $10,000. (Or your competitors are unrealistic in their pricing!)

Have I determined the inventory of unsold houses?

It's important to get a handle on where the market is when you put your home up for sale. If there's a surplus of housing available, it's unlikely you'll be able to get top dollar for your house. Indeed, prices may be softening and you may be lucky to get what comparables sold for last year. On the other hand, if there are shortages in the market (more buyers than homes for sale), prices should be stiffening, meaning you can get more for your property. The key, of course, is learning the true supply/demand status for your area. By the way, statistics thrown out by the media are usually not very helpful in that they typically give national or state figures on housing supplies. However, all real estate is local. What should concern you is the housing situation in your area, even your neighborhood. You can determine this by checking out the inventory of unsold homes. Again, an agent can easily provide you with this information. All real estate boards keep track of how many homes are currently listed. That's called the inventory of unsold homes. The higher the inventory, the softer the market. The lower the inventory, the hotter the market. (Sometimes this statistic is given in terms of how long it will take to sell out the inventory, for example, there are 6 month's worth of houses in inventory, or 18 months, or 2 months.) While it's important to know that a low number is better (for sellers) than a higher number, it's even more important to compare the inventory today and where it was 6 months, 1 year, 2 years, and 3 years ago. By comparing today's inventory with the past, you can very quickly see the trend—is a housing shortage or surplus developing? Will I do better by selling quickly before prices soften, or by waiting until they firm? Checking inventory is a great way of not only determining the present state of the housing market in your area, but estimating future trends as well.

Have I considered the economy?

You'll almost never hear economists saying that the economy is moving along just fine. Usually it's getting better… or worse. And that can affect what you'll be able to get from your house and how you should price it. Think jobs. A healthy economy means growth. More jobs mean more people who can afford to buy houses or who want to move up to bigger and better homes. Of course, as with inventory, what counts is what's happening in your area. If you're in Seattle and Boeing, Microsoft, and others are laying people off, chances are the housing market is set to take a tumble. If you're in Los Angeles and small businesses are growing at a rapid rate and are hiring furiously, chances are housing prices are going to go up. You can find out about your local economy just by reading the local newspaper on a regular basis—the media loves to focus on it. Check also with your local Chamber of Commerce, although you can expect them to give the best possible slant on local conditions. If you want some technical insight, check with a local college that has an economics department. It may have issued a "White Paper" on the subject, or even may refer you to a professor who would be willing to spend a few minutes on the phone explaining his or her perspective. Finally, use what I use—the Franchise Food Barometer. McDonald's, Burger King, Wendy's, Chili's, and all the dozens of other franchise food establishments pay economists millions of dollars to tell them where to put their restaurants. They want to go into areas of growth, where the economy is booming, where more and more people are moving who are likely to use their facilities. Thus, if there's a lot of franchise food growth in your area, it suggests a very healthy economy. On the other hand, if no new franchise food restaurants are opening—indeed some of the existing ones are closing—it suggests a local economy in the dumps.

Have I factored in interest rates?

Real estate is interest-rate sensitive. Simply put, when mortgage interest rates go down, sales pick up because more buyers can afford to purchase homes… and bigger homes. When interest rates go up, sales go down because fewer buyers can afford to purchase homes… or to move to other homes. If you are fortunate enough to be selling during a time when interest rates are falling, you most likely will see prices climbing. If you're not averse to risk-taking, you may even want to play the market by holding your home off the market until rates fall lower. (Of course, there's always the chance they could change direction, wherein lies the risk.) On the other hand, if rates are high or rising when you try to sell, expect it to take longer to find a buyer and to get a softer price. Of course, the more dramatic the change in mortgage interest rates, the greater the effect on the market. For example, back in the late 1970s when interest rates rose as high as 17 to 18 percent, housing sales virtually came to a halt. During 2003, on the other hand, when rates fell to 5 percent, the market boomed. By the way, it's mortgage interest rates that count, not short-term bonds. While mortgage rates do depend on bond rates, particularly the long bond, they don't always move exactly in tandem. Indeed, the interest rate on long-term bonds is more of a prognosticator of future mortgage rates than an indicator of current rates.

How price sensitive are buyers?

Very. This is an important concept sometimes lost on sellers. For example, after going through all of the analyses noted above, you may determine that the correct asking price to set for your home is $300,000. However, you'd really like to get more, say $310,000 or at least $307,000. So you put your home up for sale at $307,000. After all, you say to yourself, what have I got to lose? If somebody offers you $290,000 (probably the expected selling price—remember sales price is usually lower than asking price), you can still take it. On the other hand, you might just catch a buyer who'll pay more. Sound like a reasonable gambit? But it's not. Buyer's are very price sensitive and after looking around for awhile, they'll get very good at determining what the correct *asking* price should be. They'll realize that it should be $300,000 in your case. But, you're asking too much. Very likely they are thinking to themselves that you're an unrealistic seller, one who doesn't understand values, one who will be hard to deal with, one who won't sell for what the house is truly worth. A headache. Therefore, they pass you by. They don't make those offers that they would otherwise make on your home. And as a result, your property sits there, unsold. By raising your price even just 2 percent or so higher than it should be, you've taken yourself out of the market. You've stopped being a player. How much higher is too much? Sometimes it can be as little as 1 percent above market. The closer you can price your home to market, the quicker you're going to get it sold. This is why "range" pricing has come into existence. (See below.)

What price can I realistically get?

That, of course, is the ultimate question. You don't want to price your home too high and miss the market. On the other hand, you don't want to ask too little and miss out on cash you can make. My suggestion is you do the analyses noted above. You also should ask several agents for their best estimate of your home's worth. (Remember, however, agents have a vested interest in telling you what they think you want to hear, hoping that you'll list with them.) If you have to err, my suggestion is that you err on the side of pricing a little bit too high. Remember, you may be able to generate new interest in your home later on with a price cut.

Can I afford to sell?

This is a completely different question from what price you should ask. It's important to keep the two separate. Sales price and what you can afford to sell for are two distinct things. What you can afford to sell your home for depends on the following:

- How much you currently owe (payoffs) on all your mortgages,
- How much it will cost in transaction fees (commission and other closing costs), and
- How much you need out of your equity in your home.

However, while all of the above are very important to you, they are irrelevant to a buyer. A buyer doesn't care what you owe, or what it will cost you to sell, or even what you think your equity should be. A buyer is only concerned in getting a good deal and that's usually defined as buying a home at or below market price. Thus, you'll need to see how much you can get for your house. And then compare this figure with what it will cost you to sell and what you hope to get out of the sale. You might discover that it just doesn't pay you to sell at this point. You could even find, as did many homesellers during the real estate recession of the 1990s, that you're "upside down," it costs more to sell than the property is worth. Making the decision to sell/not sell often hinges on whether or not the market will allow you to get what you want out of your house.

Should I call in an appraiser?

Appraisers are rarely used to help set prices on residential real estate. They are used extensively by mortgage lenders to set valuations on which to base loans and to set prices on commercial and industrial property. Using them for homes, condos, and co-ops is kind of overkill. Besides, in my experience more likely than not the appraiser will come in with the wrong market price! That's not to say that appraisers don't do a good job. They do. However, they typically only consider comparables—*past* sales of similar properties. Thus, by nature, their valuations tend to be conservative. The most dramatic example of this I've ever seen was in some recreational property in the mountains. A neighboring owner called in an appraiser to see what her home was worth. This was in an area of custom homes that seldom sold, so it was difficult to find comparable sales nearby. As a result, the appraiser went several miles away to where several homes had recently sold. He came back with an appraised value of $165,000. However, the market was booming in the area where the seller's property was located, so discounting the appraisal, the seller put her home up for sale at $250,000. It sold within a week! (She later complained she had sold it for too little!) If you want an appraisal, for about $350 an appraiser can put the "official" stamp on the value of your property. However, I'm not sure you can't do as good a job, if not better, of determining price on your own.

QUESTIONS TO ASK AN AGENT

Can you give me a CMA?

A comparative market analysis looks at other comparable homes that have recently sold in your area and, allowing for differences, comes up with a price that your home will likely sell for. Any good agent should be able to prepare this for you. Some agents will do a fancy job putting it together in a little folder with a cover. I prefer, however, an agent who sits down with you at his or her computer and begins calling up all the comparable homes, then going through each one, feature by feature (square footage, bedrooms and bathrooms, lot size, features, and so on) so that you can see exactly how your home is both similar and different and in this way get a good sense of how the selling price is determined. Of course, remember, that while useful, a CMA is not the final answer. You also will want to ask your agent about inventories, prices of homes currently for sale, the spread between asking and selling price, the economy, mortgage interest rates, and all the other factors affecting price.

Do you suggest absentee pricing?

This is a trick that agents sometimes suggest in order to stir up a buying frenzy resulting in a higher price. It basically works by holding the home off the market, at the same time it's offered for sale. The trick is to list the home, promote it, ask for offers, and then not respond to them. It's most commonly done by having the sellers leave for a 7-14-day cruise immediately upon listing the property. When a buyer makes an offer, the listing agent simply says the seller is away on a cruise and unreachable. The buyer will simply have to wait until the seller returns. When a second offer comes in, the second buyer is told the same thing, in addition to the fact that there's already an offer on the property. Now there are two buyers who have plenty of time to become anxious. Both may be thinking about increasing their bid in order to get the house. If a third buyer appears on the scene, you've got a feeding frenzy. Each buyer, worrying about the others, may begin increasing the bid. (*Note:* Normally, one buyer won't know what another is bidding and a seller's agent won't—or shouldn't—tell them, but a buyer's agent sometimes can find out and will tell his or her client.) In some cases the bid prices have far exceeded the asking price. When the sellers return, they simply accept the highest bid, presumably more than they could otherwise have gotten. Of course, besides being unethical, it also should be noted that this is only likely to work in a very hot market. If the market is misjudged, the seller may miss out on a perfectly good offer that a buyer withdraws after learning that the seller claims not to be available. (After all, in this day and age of FAXes, cell phones, the Internet, and overnight shipping, how can anyone on the planet not be available within a few hours?!) I would discourage you from using this technique unless you fully understand the risks.

Do You Suggest Underpricing?

This is another similar trick that agents sometimes (unethically, in my opinion) suggest to stir up a buying frenzy and get a higher price. It's remarkable in that when it works, it accomplishes exactly the opposite of what it seems to. Here, you deliberately underprice your home. For example, your house may be worth $400,000 at market. But instead of asking that price, you ask $375,000 or even $350,000. You list it at that price and put it on the MLS®. Now, as above, you leave for a few days. (Remember, you're conveniently unavailable.) As we've noted, buyers are very price conscious. It won't take long for buyers to realize that some fool seller has put a house up for sale way under market. Immediately you can expect to get some full-price offers. (After all, at full price the house is a steal.) But, as soon as one buyer sees another making an offer, he or she will likely want to up the bidding. After all, it's a steal! Very quickly there could be half a dozen buyers bidding the price up. Soon the price is escalating, you hope, even above market price. When you return, you find you're accepting an offer for much more. At least you hope so. However, this technique is even more fraught with peril for the unfortunate seller. When it doesn't work (which is usually in all but the hottest of markets), you may be caught into accepting a lower-than-market offer. Perhaps only one buyer made an offer at your full, low price. No, you don't have to accept. But if you don't, you're possibly liable for a full commission. While your agent who may suggest this strategy may not demand this commission, a buyer's agent who came in with the full-price offer almost certainly will. It's something to consider before agreeing to underprice your home.

Do you suggest range-pricing?

This technique has only come into play in the last few years. Here, instead of asking a single price for your home, you ask a range of prices. For example, instead of asking $400,000, you ask a low of $375,000 to a higher of $415,000. You'll entertain any offer in that price range. It is used when sellers really want/hope to get more than the market value of their home. They are asking for high bids, indicating that they will entertain low offers if no high bids come in. Of course, most buyers find this insulting, if not ridiculous. Smart buyers already realize that every home on the market is for sale in a range of prices. Typically the seller asks the maximum and buyers offer what they think is reasonable. When you buy a new car, the sticker price is right on the window for all to see. Yet, any savvy buyer knows that he or she can offer any price for it, and often the sale price is below the sticker price. (Interestingly, when you buy a used car, the true asking price is sometimes hard to find.) The problem here is that in any but the hottest market, you're more likely to get a lot of lowball offers than any high ones. Buyers tend to focus on the lowest price you list. If your agent suggests listing your property at range-pricing, be sure you thoroughly question him or her on what recent success they've had with this technique. And ask to be shown how many houses currently on the market offer it. Then, before you agree, reconsider the risks.

What, in your opinion, is my house really worth?

It's not a trick question. Rather, you're asking for the real estate agent's opinion based, presumably, on years of selling property. And chances are excellent that a good agent can step into your house, walk around it for a few minutes, and come up with a price that will be within dollars of its market value. They know, or should know, what your home should sell for based on their experience in the marketplace. I've done this myself when selling residential property. Before going out to see a seller to get a listing, I'd get the address of the house and verify the comparables. Of course, I already knew the area (which was my "farm"—where I worked real estate). Then, I'd go see the seller and take a quick tour of the home, and adjust the price according to its condition. Of course, I'd present a CMA, talk about economics, jobs, mortgage interest rates, housing shortages, price trends, and so on before finally coming up with a price. But, I could just as easily have given them this price after just a quick look at the property. It comes from being in the business year in and year out. Therefore, simply asking the agent what the right price should be can save a lot of time. Of course, you won't know it's the correct price for sure, until you go through all the steps yourself.

What can I do to improve my home's for-sale value?

Agents can be very helpful here. Almost certainly they will suggest cleaning, painting, and fixing (see Chapter 1). Some excellent agents will even have a crew of cleaners on call who will come into your house for a few hours and do a whirlwind cleaning of it for you! Beyond this, they may discover some problem areas of your home, areas that you weren't aware of. For example, they may say your home is too dark—add more lighting fixtures and be sure to leave them on when showing the home. Or they may point out that a room divider makes the house look small—remove it. Or they could suggest adding mirrors to walls and closet doors to make your home look bigger. Or they may simply tell you to park your old car one block over when buyers come by! Don't assume you already know what an agent will tell you about improving your home to help sell it. Almost all sellers are surprised at what agents can find.

How long do you think it will take to sell my home?

After price, this is the next question that almost all sellers ask agents. After all, once you've listed the house you want to get on with it... get it sold! Of course, most agents are going to hem and haw a bit. They'll say something like, "We'll try to get it sold quickly." Some will even say, "Better be prepared to move soon!" While the truth of the matter is that no one can say for sure how long it will take to find a buyer, active agents usually have a good idea of the time based on recent market sales. If listed homes have been selling within a week or two, they'll tell you. Or, if it's been taking 6 to 9 months, they'll tell you that, too. Yes, you can check the housing inventory in your area. But sometimes a more accurate estimate can be given off the cuff by a good agent.

Should I get a formal appraisal?

As noted earlier, a formal appraisal of residential real estate for the purpose of setting a price is of limited value. Expect most agents to tell you this. However, sometimes there are special circumstances, as when you have a unique house (it's round instead of square, comes with a lot of acreage, could have industrial usage value, and so on) and an agent may indicate that an "official" appraisal could be worthwhile. On the other hand, beware of an agent who wants to charge you for an appraisal. Appraisers do not usually act as real estate agents and vice versa. Rather, appraisers are their own breed. They usually belong to a national appraisal organization such as the MAI or SREA (see the Resources section at the end of this book), and they may be licensed as appraisers in your state. They probably have taken extensive educational courses in appraisal and usually have served an apprenticeship learning how to correctly appraise property. They are professionals. On the other hand, when an average agent wants to charge you for an appraisal he or she is doing, without the above qualifications, you are probably just wasting your money. And you have to ask yourself why an agent, presumably successful in selling property, needs to charge a client for an appraisal? Remember, virtually all agents offer a CMA for free.

4
Checking Out the Agreement When You List

QUESTIONS TO ASK YOURSELF

Have I decided on a price?

Any real estate agent with whom you deal will be happy to help you come up with a price. But, it's a better idea if you decide on the realistic price you want before contacting an agent, before putting your home up for sale. (If you're not sure about how to do this, reread Chapter 3.) That's not to say you shouldn't listen carefully to the price your agent suggests and the arguments given to justify it. It's just that if you do your own homework, check out the market and the competition, then you're going to feel a whole lot better about the price you ask. It's usually a lot better to trust yourself than to rely on the judgment of others.

Have I decided on a commission rate?

The most frequent answer to this is, "Yes, and it's 1 percent!" Nobody wants to pay a hefty commission to someone else. After all, it's money right out of your pocket. However, if you want to get your home sold, and you don't want the considerable chore of trying to sell it yourself, you're going to have to hire an agent… and pay a commission. While going for the smallest commission possible sounds good, it's worthwhile putting the shoe on the other foot, just for size. If you were the agent, how large a commission would you ask for the work involved?

If it seems high, ask yourself if your agent can get you a
quicker sale and a higher price; if so, it might be worth
paying a higher commission. If you plan on doing much
of the selling work yourself, then obviously a lower
commission is more realistic. Keep in mind that there is
no "set" or "minimum" commission for agents anywhere in the country. The rate is entirely between you
and your agent. However, having said that, be aware
that the most common commission rates are between 4
percent (if you do some of the sales work) and 7 percent
(for a full-service office). I think it's a good idea to
decide on the rate you are willing to pay before you
interview your agent. You can even make the rate a criteria for picking an agent. Just remember, you usually
get what you pay for.

Have I decided for how long to list?

I've never met an agent who didn't want a listing for as
long as possible. Given a choice, an agent would probably prefer to list your property until sold, even if it took
years! After all, it's the listing that ties up your property.
It's the listing that leads to the commission. No listing,
in real estate, is tantamount to being out of work. Therefore, don't be surprised if an agent says something like,
"I usually only accept listings for 6 months (or 9
months, or whatever)." However, what's good for the
agent may not necessarily be good for you. How do you
know you'll be happy with the agent's work? What if
the agent takes your listing and then disappears, never
to be heard from again? Besides, I strongly believe in
deadlines. If I have a project and 6 weeks to do it, it will
take me 6 weeks. On the other hand, if I have the same
project and I only have 6 days to do it, by gosh, I'll be
done in 6 days. Agents often are similarly inclined.
Therefore, my suggestion is to offer the agent a 3-month
listing, nothing more. Remember, if the agent does a
good job and you're happy with his or her work during
the 3 months, if the house doesn't sell, you can always
extend the listing for an additional 3 months. Oh, and
don't be put off by agents who say they won't accept
any listing of less than 6 months. Most will be very
happy to accept your 3-month listing, no matter what
they say!

Do I understand the listing agreement?

There is nothing illegal about an oral listing. However, an agent can't compel you to pay a commission based on it. According to the Statute of Frauds, most things involving real estate must be in writing to be enforceable. Hence, an agent will want you to sign a written listing agreement. This agreement may be several pages long and you should check it over carefully, perhaps even have your attorney look at it before signing it. Some of the areas to be concerned about include:

- **A specific start and termination date:** You want this date written in, not just something such as "for three months."

- **The conditions under which you will pay a commission:** For example, many listings say you owe a commission when the agent finds a buyer, "ready, willing, and able" to purchase. That can mean that while you don't have to sell to such a buyer, even if you don't sell, you could owe a commission! Some sellers have taken to changing the wording to say that a commission is due only upon the successful close of escrow (sale of the property to a buyer).

- **The amount of the commission:** Usually it's a percentage of the sale price.

- **The amount of the deposit you want:** In today's market, with deals typically not solidified until weeks after the purchase agreement has been signed, a large initial deposit is not usually necessary. But, you may require the buyer to increase the deposit after the contingencies have been removed.

- **Who gets the deposit:** Yes, it's your money and so the listing should state. However, what happens if the buyer doesn't go through with the purchase and the deposit is forfeited? In that case, most listings specify that it's split between the agent and seller. To keep everyone else in the deal from worrying, the deposit is usually held by a neutral escrow, although technically, it's usually yours as soon as the sale agreement is signed.

- **The terms you want:** Do you want all cash? Are you willing to carry a second mortgage in favor of the buyers? Careful of what you put here. If the agent brings in a buyer who meets your criteria, you might owe a commission, even if you later decide you don't like those terms.

- **The name of the agent:** If the agent is a salesperson, typically he or she will sign for their broker. The broker may need to check over the listing and sign it to make it "official."

- **What your obligations are:** Are you required to do any of the selling or paperwork? Do you have to show the property? Do you have to maintain it in any specific kind of condition?

- **What the obligations of the agent are:** Usually these include wording to the effect that the agent will work diligently to find a buyer. Few agents will agree to specifics, such as an advertising schedule.

- **Will there be a keybox:** Buyers come by when they're ready, not when you're ready. Therefore, it's a good idea to allow the agent to show the property even when you're not home. Since there may be many cooperative agents, the common way of handling this is to have a keybox installed. The listing agreement asks you to give permission for a keybox. Be aware, however, that you are opening your home up to a great many people. Agents and buyers represent a broad spectrum of people. Just as in the general population, there are those who are scrupulously honest as well as those who are dishonest. While the incidence of theft from homes with keyboxes installed is small, it does occasionally occur. Therefore, for the time you have a keybox on your home you are well advised to remove all valuables. *Note:* In many listing agreements the agents specifically disclaim responsibility for loss due to having a keybox improperly used.

- **Will the agent put a sign in the yard:** The listing agreement will ask your permission for the agent to install a reasonable sign in your front yard. It's an excellent method of attracting buyers, perhaps the best.

- **Arbitration and attorney's fees clause:** What if you have a dispute with your agent? How will it be handled. Many listings state that in the case of a lawsuit the prevailing party will have his or her attorney's costs paid by the losing party. This may be good or bad for you. Further, by signing the listing you may give up your right to call in an attorney and sue instead opting for arbitration. Read the wording carefully. You may want to ask an attorney if you should sign or change it. (Remember, if you don't agree to arbitration now, you can agree to it later on, if the other party is agreeable.)

- **Handling of disclosures:** The listing agreement also should list the various disclosures that you as a seller must make to a buyer in your state. (These are detailed in Chapter 5.)

- **An equal housing statement:** You must be in compliance with federal and state antidiscrimination laws when you list your home.

- **Transaction fee:** Watch out for this one. This is a fee that brokers have been tacking on paid directly to their office. It's often around $500. It's over and above the commission. Brokers charge this fee because they are paying their salespeople higher commissions, leaving less for their overhead. However, that's their problem, not yours. I wouldn't sign any listing with a transaction fee in it.

Has the agent asked for my "power-of-attorney?"

If you give someone your power-of-attorney, they can sign for you. If you give it to your agent, depending on how the document is drawn, he or she could sign the purchase agreement and other documents for you. In other words, you'd be trusting your agent to determine price and other important matters. Do you want to do this? Most agents never ask for a power-of-attorney. If your agent does, you should be sure that he or she has good reasons for doing so. (Sometimes you will want to give your power-of-attorney to a relative or close friend if you are going to be away for an extended period of time, or if you are ill and incapable of handling your own financial matters.) There are at least two types of power-of-attorney; general, in which the person can sign almost anything for you, and specific, in which he or she can only sign specific documents. It's an important document and one which you should discuss with your attorney before giving it to your agent or anyone else.

Do I get to choose title insurance and escrow companies?

Sometimes. It can be to your advantage to use a title insurance and escrow company that you used when you purchased your home, if it's only been a couple of years. The reason is that you can ask for a "reissue fee." For the same house, many title insurance/escrow companies will offer a reduced fee, provided only a few years have passed. (That's because it's easier for them to do the work involved.) However, be aware that under HUD settlement procedures, the seller may not require, as a condition of sale, that title insurance be purchased by the buyer from any particular title company. (In theory, if the seller violates this rule, he or she could be liable to the buyer for up to three times all charges made for the title insurance!) Further, sometimes the real estate agent(s) will want to use a specific title insurance and/or escrow company because it's owned by the real estate company. While kickbacks or referral fees are generally prohibited, there is a special status called a "controlled business arrangement" where the party referring the homebuyer to a provider of services has a relationship with that provider which involves an ownership or franchise. This is allowed provided the controlled business arrangement is disclosed, you're given a written estimate of costs by the provider of the service, and you are not required to use that service. Sometimes the fact that you are not required to use the controlled service might be overlooked by an overeager agent.

Has my attorney reviewed the listing?

Very few sellers actually ask their attorney to look over their listing. The assumption is that the listing is somehow not that important a document. It's not, after all, a sales agreement. It doesn't usually involve the immediate exchange of money. If the house doesn't sell and it expires, usually nothing further happens. However, this can be a fool's paradise. The listing agreement ties you into the agent and, to a certain degree, also ties you into the kind of sales offer you're likely to get. There could be clauses in it that could cost you money that you might not feel you ought to spend. However, once you sign, you could be on the hook. Therefore, you should have your attorney check it over.

QUESTIONS TO ASK AN AGENT

For how long do you want to take a listing?

While some agents will come right out and say they'll list your property for 3 months, some (as noted earlier) will demand a longer term. Why? I'd suspect three possible reasons: First, they simply aren't sure of themselves and are worried they won't be able to perform in just 3 months; second, they aren't sure of the market and fear that it may simply be too difficult to find a buyer in such a short time; or third, they know you've priced your home too high and are hoping that over time you'll reduce it to a more realistic level, hence, they aren't going to do very much for you during the early months of the listing. If the agent is unsure, then tell him or her that you'll be happy to renew the listing at the end of the first 3 months, if you've seen that they've tried hard, but the market is just cold. On the other hand, if it's because your home is priced too high, then reconsider the price. What's the point of wasting time trying to get an unrealistic price? Ask the agent to be candid about the value of your property. And be sure to confirm a lower value by rechecking the comparables (see Chapter 3).

Are you happy with my listing?

You don't want an unhappy camper. Your agent says she never accepts a listing for less than 6 months. You offer 3 months. She accepts and then grumbles that she just won't have time to do a good job on your listing, that it's hardly worth her efforts signing you up, that signing you up is just a charitable effort on her part. Stop. Don't finish writing up the listing. Don't sign. Show this agent to the door. Regardless of the term of the listing (or the commission rate), once agreed upon, you want your agent upbeat, enthusiastic, and positive about finding a buyer. That's what you should expect and if you get anything less, it may just mean that this agent isn't planning to do a good job for you. And if she isn't going to work hard, why bother with her? After all, keep in mind there is no shortage of excellent real estate agents out there, any of whom would be delighted to accept a 3-month listing from you.

What kind of listing do you want?

Contrary to what some people think, there are actually many different types of listing agreements, each of which grants the agent specific rights and limitations. You should ask your agent what type he or she prefers and be sure you understand the ramifications of each before signing. Here are the most popular:

- An *exclusive right-to-sell listing* is the type that almost all agents prefer. It is also the type that many listing services, such as the MLS, may demand. It means the following: If the agent or anyone else (including you) sells the house, you owe the agent a commission. This includes people to whom you showed the house while the listing was in effect, even though you sold the house (for a period of time) after the listing had expired. In other words, with this type of listing you ensure the agent a commission if the house is sold. About the only way the agent cannot get a commission is if there is no sale. Sellers tend to dislike this type of commission because they feel it's unfair. Agents, on the other hand, like it because they feel protected. Most are willing to put forth 100 percent effort only if they get this type of listing. I believe it is the one most likely to get you the most action on your property.

- An *exclusive agency listing* is a watered down version of the one above. If the agent sells the house, you owe a commission. If you yourself sell it to someone the agent didn't show it to, you don't owe anything. Agents have good reasons for not liking this type of listing. They may bring buyers to your home who tell them they're not interested in purchasing. Later, the buyers come to you and negotiate a sale. You claim no commission is due because you had no knowledge that the agent showed these buyers the home; they dealt directly with you. The agent claims that a commission is due because he or she found the buyer. In this case, the agent is right. But to get that commission the agent might have to go to arbitration or even to court. Along the way there's certain to be hard feelings, and agents are very concerned about their reputation in a community. They don't like it to be known that they're having to put pressure on a client to collect even a justified commission. Thus, most agents simply won't work (or won't work as hard) for you on this type of listing.

- In an *open listing* you agree to pay a commission to any broker who brings you a buyer or to pay no commission if you find the buyer. Some sellers think this is a good type of listing because you can give it to any agent. Most agents, however, won't devote 10 minutes of time to this kind of listing. If buyers should show up whom they can't interest in any other piece of property, then they'll bring them to you in a last-chance effort at a commission. The opportunity to do work and not get paid for it is so great here that agents in general just don't want to bother with this type of listing. About the only time it's used is in bare land, when the chances of selling are very slim and it could take years to produce a buyer. You might simply let every agent know that the property is for sale and you'll pay a commission, but you're not willing to give any one of them an "exclusive."

- Sometimes agents will offer you a *guaranteed-sale listing*. A guaranteed-sale listing isn't a separate type of listing. Rather, it's any of the above but is

usually the exclusive right to sell. The listing
simply includes a separate clause which says
that if the property isn't sold by the end of the
listing term, then the agent agrees to buy it from
you for a set price (usually the listing price), less
the commission. While this sounds like a
panacea, you should be careful with it. Although
widely used at one time, this type of listing is
often frowned upon today because of the potential conflict of interest. The reason is simple.
While an honest agent can use the guaranteed-
sale listing to induce you to list, a dishonest
agent can use it to gain a larger-than-expected
commission. A dishonest agent may induce an
unwary seller to list, then take no action to sell
the property. When the listing expires, the agent
buys the house at a previously guaranteed lower
price and later resells at a much higher price.
This is particularly a problem when the listing
calls for the agent to buy the property for less
than the listed price (justified by the supposed
"fact" that because it didn't sell for the listed
price, ergo, that price was too high). If your
agent suggests this type of listing, insist on the
following (which may already be legally
required in your state):

1. The agent can buy the property only for the
    listed price. No less.
2. The agent has to inform you, and you have to
    agree in writing, if the agent resells the prop-
    erty to someone else within 1 year of your
    sale to the agent.
3. The agent must buy the property. The agent
    can't sell it to a third party in escrow, unless
    you get all the proceeds less the agreed upon
    commission.

- A *net listing* is by far the most controversial type.
  And I would be wary of any agent who insists
  on it. With a net listing, you agree up front on a
  fixed price for the property. Everything over that
  price goes to the agent. You agree to sell for
  $100,000. If the agent brings in a buyer for
  $105,000, the agent gets $5000 as the commission. But if the agent brings in a buyer for

$150,000 the agent gets $50,000 for a commission! The opportunities to take advantage of a seller here should be obvious. An unscrupulous agent could get a listing for a low price and then sell for a high one, getting an unconscionable commission. On the other hand, a net listing is sometimes useful for a "hopeless" property. For one reason or another, the property isn't salable. So the seller tells the agent, "Be creative. Find a buyer. Here's what I want. Everything else is yours." In such an arrangement, you as the seller should insist (if state law doesn't already require it) that you be informed of the final selling price and that you agree in writing to it. The easiest way to handle a net listing is to simply avoid it.

Will you co-broke my property with other agents?

Here you're asking your agent if he or she plans on holding your property off the market, that is, away from other agents so he or she can sell it themselves. Or, is the agent willing to co-broke, or cooperate, with all the other agents in the area? Be wary if the agent tells you something like, "To give you a better chance at a quick sale, I'll hold back the listing from the cooperative listing service for a few weeks. This means that all the agents in my office will work harder on it. It's really a better opportunity for you as the seller." It's actually a ploy to give the listing agent a chance to sell your property exclusively without having to split the commission. During those few weeks before your house gets on the cooperative system, your agent may indeed be knocking himself out trying to sell it. But that's one agent. On the service, as many as 1000 or more agents will be aware that your house is for sale. One of them may already have a buyer looking for just what you've got. Don't let the agent "hold back" or "vest pocket" your listing. Insist that it be given the widest possible exposure at the soonest possible time.

If you are an independent, will you list on the MLS?

In this day and age most agents belong to large companies which often franchise offices (although some are wholly owned) such as Coldwell-Banker, Prudential, Century 21, RE/MAX, and so on. On the other hand, there are still many independent and highly successful offices, particularly in smaller communities. If you're thinking of listing with an independent, be sure they belong to the MLS and will list your house on it. This allows all the other brokers (chain as well as independent) to work on it. Keep in mind, however, that real estate is a very personal business. What counts most is the person with whom you are dealing, whether an independent or a chain. If you get a good agent, stick with him or her.

Are you a REALTOR®?

This is an agent who belongs to the National Association of REALTORS (NAR). REALTOR is a copyrighted term and only NAR members may use it. Also, most real estate boards are affiliated with the NAR and, hence, nonmembers may not be able to list property on the MLS. Besides, this is an excellent trade organization that worked hard for years to upgrade the profession, so why wouldn't you want to deal with an agent member?

If you are a chain, what advantages will you offer me?

A real estate chain offers name recognition, sometimes better advertising support, office management help, standard forms, and a measure of assurance to you that if something goes wrong, hopefully there's a big entity out there to save your bacon. That may or may not be true, depending on the office. However, chains offer at least a minimal standard of performance. One office tends to look like another, and in general, the agents tend to be fairly well trained. In addition, chains offer long-distance moving assistance. List your home with a chain in one city and an agent from a linked chain in another city can already be looking for a new home for you. In my opinion, the true value of the chain is that it brings a degree of order, of homogeneity, to real estate.

What commission rate do you want?

This, of course, is the big question. You ask it and the agent will tell you. However, no matter what the agent says, remember that in real estate, everything is negotiable. If the agent says 7 percent (or, worse, 8 percent!), that doesn't mean you have to accept. Take what the agent initially demands as the starting point for negotiations, and try to work downward from there. The agent asks 7 or 8 percent, you offer 4. Is there room to compromise? Some agents won't. They'll tell you they are worth every penny of what they ask and they're so busy they simply won't (or don't need to) accept less. If the agent is adamant, then if you think he or she is worthwhile, pay it. Otherwise, look elsewhere. Remember, the commission is whatever you finally say it is. It's not what the agent demands it to be. However, don't be pennywise and pound foolish. If you negotiate an agent down to a level where he or she grudgingly takes your listing, you may have just guaranteed a long wait for a sale. This agent may simply put your listing on the back burner and not work it. Try to find middle ground. Find a listing rate both you and the agent can live with.

Is there a transaction fee?

Don't forget to ask this question. And read the listing agreement carefully to be sure it's not in there. A transaction fee is a charge to you over and above the commission. It can be as high as $500, sometimes more. It goes directly to the agent's office, usually bypassing the agent. Some offices have instituted it because they're paying their top agents such high splits (80 percent in some cases) that they can't afford to stay in business otherwise. So, they're trying to get the money from the client. However, you are under no obligation to bail out the listing office. How they do business is their business, not yours. I would insist that any transaction fee be deleted from the listing. If the agent refuses (or says that his or her broker won't accept a listing without it), then remind that agent how many other agents are beating down your door to get your listing. By the way, beware if you do sign a listing with the transaction fee in it. It will crop up again at closing, and you may be obligated to pay it because you agreed to it in the listing.

Is there a title company/escrow company you insist on using?

Agents will often have favorites. They may have worked with the escrow officer and know that he or she does a good job. This is important because an unreliable escrow officer can mess up a deal in ways you wouldn't believe possible. If you trust your agent (and you should) and he or she has strong feelings about a particular title insurance and/or escrow company, then I'd seriously consider using it. On the other hand, if there's an advantage to you of using a particular company (such as getting a lower "reissue" fee—see above), then by all means bring this out. The agent should be willing to compromise to save you money. Also, it wouldn't hurt to ask the agent if his or her company has any relationship to the title insurance/escrow company.

Who pays for title insurance and escrow charges?

These can be substantial fees running into the thousands of dollars. However, the division of who pays them is often made by local custom. In some areas the buyer is responsible. In other areas the seller. Today, increasingly, they are split between buyer and seller. If it turns out that in your area the seller usually pays, ask the agent if he or she can negotiate with a potential buyer to pay, or at least, split the costs. You may even want to incorporate this into your listing agreement.

What if I do some of the work?

Agents are usually adamant about the services they perform. Either they are full-service brokerages, or they aren't. If they are, they will tell you to sit back and relax. They'll handle it from here. Indeed, they may not want your interference in doing a job they feel very professional about. On the other hand, if you're dealing with a reduced commission agency, they may be expecting you to handle some of the workload. Better find out now what's expected of you, as it may be written into the listing. You might be responsible for showing your property, for paying for some or all advertising, for clearing "clouds" or items on the title to your property that affect its merchantability. You might decide that there's too much work for you, and prefer to go back to a full-service agent. Or the reverse can be true. It's important to get this out and on the table early on.

What type of listing will you want?

As noted earlier, expect the agent to want an exclusive right to sell. That means that he or she gets paid no matter who sells the property, even if it's you. There are good reasons to give agents this type of listing as it helps ensure you'll get hard work out of them. On the other hand, you may have a buyer whom you've been working with for several weeks, but who simply hasn't made the decision to purchase. You may insist on excluding this buyer from the listing, turning it into an exclusive agency listing. You'll pay the agent for selling to any buyers, except those to whom you sell directly. Or maybe the agent comes to you with a specific buyer in mind. He or she says that this buyer wants to see your house, but the agent won't show it unless and until you sign a listing agreement. There's nothing to prevent you from signing a 1-day or 1-week listing. If the agent really can produce such a buyer, you may be willing to give them a commission. But, if after a reasonable time (a day, a week, or whatever), nothing develops, the listing is over. Remember, you can negotiate the listing agreement.

Do you offer a guaranteed-sale listing?

Most agents won't, but some will. As noted earlier, this essentially means that if they can't sell your home by the time the listing expires, they'll buy it. If the agent offers this type of listing, be sure they'll buy it for the listed sale price (less the commission). If they offer to buy it for less, you have to wonder if you haven't listed your home for too high a price. Also, be sure that they specify who will pay the closing costs and that they aren't heaped on you. And finally, it's a good idea to insist that they get your approval before reselling the property within 6 months or a year. This is to ensure that they aren't "flipping" you, buying with the intent of quickly reselling at a higher amount for a big profit.

Who gets any forfeited deposit?

Usually it's split between seller and agent. But it doesn't have to be. You can insist that it all be given to you. Most agents, however, will just as adamantly insist on splitting, as this is a long tradition in the industry. Beware of an agent who insists that he or she gets it all!

5
Preparing Disclosures

QUESTIONS TO ASK YOURSELF

Do I know what disclosures are?

□

Disclosures in real estate refer to the practice of telling buyers of your home about defects of which you are aware (or should be aware). The purpose here is to ensure that buyers know more precisely what they are getting. Given the large sums of money involved in a home purchase, the intent is to see that buyers make offers based not simply on the superficial appearance of a home but rather on its actual condition. In the old days (read several decades ago), many sellers preferred not to disclose this vital information preferring instead to believe that *caveat emptor* (let the buyer beware) prevails. In other words, they felt that it's up to the buyer to find problems, not up to the seller to disclose them. However, in recent years lawsuits by buyers over defects in homes have made it plain that disclosing defects is an important part of nearly all real estate transactions and a seller who fails to do so is at risk.

What can happen if I don't disclose defects?

□

Buyers may sue sellers over undisclosed defects that the sellers know about, or should have known about. They can claim that the sellers covered up or hid defects in order to get a higher, and perhaps unrealistic, price. In some severe cases, the buyers may even sue the seller for rescission, demanding that the sellers take back the house and return the money to the buyers. And, of course, there's always the prospect of additional damages. Given the added fact that most home purchases involve a lender and large loans, this can be a real nightmare. Finally, nearly all states have now incorporated disclosures into their real estate code, which means that failure to disclose might constitute breaking the law.

Do I need a special disclosure form?

You might. Some states specify exactly what you must disclose and, hence, those items must be in the form you use. Usually a real estate agent can provide you with a form that's appropriate for your home state. However, there may be many additional items that you'd want to disclose. And if your state doesn't require a special form, you may want to have a good agent and/or attorney prepare one for you to use.

When should I give my disclosures to the buyer?

Preferably as early as possible. That means you may want to give the disclosure to potential buyers even before they make their offer. In California, for example, buyers have a 3-day right of refusal starting when you give them the disclosures. Thus, no matter how far you may be into the deal, they can back out within 3 days of getting the disclosures by disapproving them. In other words, if you wait until after you've signed a deal and are in escrow, it can fall apart when the sellers see the disclosures. Thus, most agents try to give disclosures to the buyers at the time they prepare the purchase agreement.

Should I give my disclosures in writing?

Absolutely yes. Simply telling the buyer about the home's defects is not enough. You need a paper trail so later on, should the buyer have an attack of memory loss, you can point out exactly what and when you disclosed. And be sure the buyers date and sign for receipt of the disclosures, for the same reason.

What sorts of things must I disclose?

You normally need to disclose any and all defects in the property. For example, if your roof leaks, you should disclose it. Failure to do so can be costly. The buyer may purchase the home assuming the roof is fine. But at the first

rainfall, torrents come down into the house—you neg-
lected to mention that it leaks. You can be fairly sure that
the buyer is going to come back at you not just to fix the
leaks, but for a new roof. Of course, some sellers will
argue that they didn't know about the leaks. However,
roofers can usually tell whether a leak is new or has been
there a long time. In addition, you may need to disclose
problems that you should know about, but may not. For
example, you've smelled gas occasionally in the home,
but never did anything about it. It could be argued that a
reasonable person should have called in a plumber, or at
least a gas company technician, to check it out. Saying
you meant to, but never got around to it (and didn't disclose the gas odor), isn't going to help much if the home
explodes a month after you sell it. You need to disclose
anything that affects the value of the property, especially
items relating to health and safety.

What if I take a chance on not getting caught?

Some sellers liken this to speeding in a car. They figure
that the odds of a cop catching them are pretty remote,
hence they'll take a chance and go over the limit. However, while the police are few and far between when it
comes to catching speeders, when selling a house the
buyers are, presumably, going to be living in it full time.
If there's a problem, chances are excellent they will find it.
Hence, your odds of getting caught when there's something seriously wrong (the sort of thing that many sellers
want to avoid disclosing because it will affect the price)
are actually pretty strong. Remember, once you move out
and the buyers move in, they have total access to the
property. That not only includes living in it, but nosing
around in all its corners.

What if I play hardball and refuse to fix a problem I didn't disclose?

The buyers call up and complain that the water heater
broke just a month after they moved in, and you didn't
disclose any problem with it. They want you, the seller, to
fix it. You refuse. Chances are you might get away with it.
A new water heater costs $500 and it's probably easier for
the buyers to simply replace it than hassle you for it. If
they do decide to go after you for the money and take you
to small claims court, you can always say you didn't

know that the water heater was bad... and besides, those things can go out at anytime. (On the other hand, if the buyers produce a plumber who says he or she told you the heater was ready to drop dead just days before you sold the property, it's a different story.) On the other hand, the more money involved, often the greater the potential risk to you. If you fail to disclose severe cracks in the foundation and the house breaks in half a month after the sale and it's going to cost $75,000 to fix it, the sellers are likely to be more determined, and they may take you to court and demand not only that you fix the problem, but pay damages as well. My suggestion is that if you want to sleep well at night, you disclose everything.

Am I better off not disclosing small problems?

What do you consider small? In the question above it was the difference between a bad water heater and a bad foundation—was either small? On the other hand, it could simply be a bad fence. The fence may look straight, but you know that termites have eaten away most of the posts below ground. It's ready to fall over at any moment. Disclose this or not? When I had this situation in a home I was selling, I disclosed it. The buyers didn't like it, but it didn't keep them from buying, or influence the price. They figured it was something they'd have to fix when they moved in. My neighbor on one side, however, who sold about the same time, failed to disclose the problem. And after the sale he ended up paying for a new fence, which at $20 a foot was no small charge. My philosophy is to disclose everything. Most buyers will respect you for it. And unless it's a serious problem, it probably won't affect the sale or the price.

Should I fix the problem myself?

Sometimes. First, you have to know the problem exists. If it's water pooling under the house, you're probably well aware of it. On the other hand, if there's a problem with the electrical system, you may live in the house for years and simply be unaware of it. (Lack of a grounding wire, for example, can be a safety issue, yet might not cause trouble for a long time.) Once you know the problem, you have to decide whether or not to sell the home "as is" disclosing the problem, or to fix it. The advantages to fixing it are that:

- You won't scare away any buyers with an "as is" condition in your contract. (Some buyers are very wary of this and it can cause you to have to accept a lower price.)

- You can do it on your terms—at your convenience, choosing the contractor to handle it, and determining the extent of the fix (thus controlling the cost).

- You may be able to do the work yourself. If you wait until it's sold, on the other hand, the buyer is likely to press for a quick, expensive, professional fix.

On the other hand, sometimes giving the buyers the option of handling the fix can have its own advantages. For example, water damage has ruined the paint in a room. You fix the leak, but leave the room undone allowing a buyer to choose the room color.

Should I disclose a problem I've fixed?

Normally you should. The danger is that the fix could break and the problem could come back again. If it does, it might anger a buyer enough to go after you. On the other hand, if you disclose what the problem was and how it was remedied, and the buyer accepts that, you're probably on safer ground. Sometimes for small fixes, of course, no disclosure may need be made. For example, it's hardly worth it to disclose that you've fixed the washer in a faucet or that you've changed a broken sprinkler head (unless they reveal a broken faucet which happens to be a very expensive model or a broken watering system).

Is there a time limit for disclosures?

That depends on how disclosures are handled in your state. Some areas suggest three years as a limit beyond which you needn't disclose a minor problem. On the other hand, a serious problem, such as a cracked and fixed foundation, might need to be disclosed indefinitely. Check with an agent and attorney in your area.

Should I order my own home inspection?

Normally a buyer will order and pay for a professional home inspection (see Chapter 6 on home inspection). However, sometimes it can be to your benefit if you order it yourself even before putting your home on the market. I suggest you order this inspection if you're suspicious of a problem, but are not certain of it. A professional inspector may help dispel, or confirm, concerns here. On the other hand, if your home is relatively new and there seems to be no problems, ordering an inspection yourself can be overkill. *Note:* Buyers often will not accept an inspection report that a seller ordered. The reason is that they simply don't know if the inspector did a thorough job. They may suspect that he or she might have been your relative or a friend and, hence, did a more cursory inspection. Thus, even though you have already had a professional inspection and you provide that report to the buyers (which you should do as part of your disclosures), don't expect the buyers to reimburse you for the costs, or refrain from ordering their own inspection report.

Should I disclose a roof leak?

Yes, particularly if it's serious. Sometimes roof leaks can be annoying, but not serious. For example, even a new roof may leak around the flashing (where metal is used at junctions or valleys). It's usually just a matter of calling in a roofer who can quickly and often inexpensively fix the problem. On the other hand, you may have an older roof that really needs to be replaced. Typically, older roofs will have many leaks. Fix one and another pops up. In this case, the entire roof probably needs replacement. While you aren't expected to give the buyers a new roof, you are usually expected to give them a roof that doesn't leak, unless you disclose otherwise. Hence, you might call in a roofer to fix the leaks, but not replace the roof. (Fixing can cost hundreds of dollars—replacing can cost many thousands.) In this situation, I'd simply state that the roof leaks have been fixed (assuming they have) and that the repair was by a professional roofer. It's up to the buyers to look at it, decide if it's old and likely to leak again, and then push to negotiate the cost of a new roof.

Should I disclose a foundation crack?

I always do, even if I don't know of any cracks! Remember, repairing a foundation is probably the single most expensive fix you can make to a house. And most foundations do have cracks. These are usually minor, but you never know for sure if it's serious. (Generally "V" shaped cracks that are larger at the top than at the bottom are very serious—small hairline cracks are often nothing to be concerned about.) I usually say that there are numerous cracks in the foundation. If this alarms the buyers, they can direct their professional inspector to check it out. If none are found, or if those found are only minor, their fears are usually removed. On the other hand, I've disclosed that cracks could be there, just in case the buyers later on have problems and think about coming back at me.

Should I disclose nonpermitted additions?

I would. This refers to additions that were made without benefit of a building permit. In my experience the main reason most people put up nonpermitted additions is because they can't get approval by the building department. For example, you have a four-bedroom home and want to add an extra bedroom because of a big family. But the house is in a tract where the conditions, covenants, and restrictions (CC&Rs)—rules that go with the title—prohibit more than four bedrooms. Or perhaps you're on a septic system that allows only a maximum of four bedrooms. You can't get a permit. So you put the addition up anyway, without one. Now it's time to sell. What do you tell the buyers? I would tell them that the extra bedroom was nonpermitted. Further, I would say that if they wouldn't accept it "as is," I'd have it taken out. But won't that affect the price? It very likely could, although in most jurisdictions it's not illegal to sell a home "as is" with a nonpermitted addition. If you did a good selling job, the buyers may simply pay your price and accept it. *Note:* Doing a job "up to code" without a permit is not the same as getting a permit and having it inspected. What counts is having that piece of paper that says the building department inspected and approved the work.

Should I disclose noisy neighbors?

Unfortunately, if they're a nuisance, then you probably should. I say unfortunately because this is one of those things that's very likely to squelch a deal. Few people want to buy a home next to "bad" neighbors and if you disclose these sorts of problems, the buyers will assume (and in fact it may be true!) that you're selling to get away from the bad neighbors. On the other hand, what one person considers noisy, another may find to be no problem at all. If you don't consider your neighbors noisy, then there's probably nothing to disclose. Where problems occur is when others in the neighborhood report that your neighbor is noisy and that you've complained to them about it; when police reports show that you've filed complaints about the noisy neighbors on countless occasions; when there's public records of a lawsuit over noise between you and your neighbor. You can't claim you didn't know your neighbors were noisy if you called the police on them every week for a year.

Should I disclose barking dogs?

If the dog is right next door and if it's been keeping you awake for months, you probably should. This is particularly the case if you've regularly called the police and the animal control people about it. (See the question above.) On the other hand, dogs bark in most neighborhoods and that, in and of itself, may not be a big problem, one that you'd want to draw a buyer's attention to.

Should I disclose a death or murder in the house?

If this was 25 years ago, you probably wouldn't even ask the question. But today, it can be an issue, particularly if the person who died was murdered or died of a communicable disease (such as tuberculosis or AIDS). Buyers are squeamish about such things. Many people, for example, would not want to live in a house after a murder occurred there. They may even worry about ghosts! But more practically, they may be concerned that the death may affect their ability to sell the home in the future. There have been cases in California where buyers forced sellers into rescission because of undisclosed deaths in the home. You should disclose this even though, like noisy neighbors, this can be a deal breaker. If it is, then you may need to adjust your price accordingly to find a buyer willing to accept the "problem."

_____

Should I disclose a neighborhood problem?

It depends on the nature of the problem. If it affects the value of your property, then the answer is, yes. For example, perhaps there's a landfill nearby where toxic dumping has occurred (whether legal or illegal). Occasionally bad odors will waft out from the dump and across your property. Perhaps neighbors are concerned about toxic chemicals in the soil and water. Obviously, if you disclose all this, you're going to restrict the number of potential buyers for your home. But, it would be unethical to allow a buyer to move in unaware of the problem. More to the point, when that buyer discovered the problem, as he or she surely would, you can be quite certain they would come back to you. After all, a home near a toxic dump site is bound to be worth far less than an identical home in a toxin-free neighborhood.

_____

Should I disclose water problems?

It depends on what the problem is, but the answer is usually, an emphatic, yes. Water problems tend to be serious. These include:

- Poor drainage
- Leaking pipes
- Flooding
- Stains on walls, ceilings, or floors from previous leaks and flooding
- Standing water
- Black mold
- Other water conditions

Be aware that water problems usually fall into two categories: the first is an immediate and serious problem, such as a burst pipe or water flooding the basement.

(Modern insurance usually covers the damage, but not necessarily the cause—drying the carpet, but not fixing the broken pipe.) The second is a residual problem remaining after the initial damage such as water stains, black mold, warped boards, and so on. (Modern insurance often will not cover any of this.) Buyers deserve to be told about this, at least they will certainly think so, and they will be quite indignant if they later discover you failed to disclose. Also, keep in mind that today some insurance companies will not offer casualty insurance on any property in which there has been water damage! Without this insurance, your buyer might not be able to get a mortgage, or you might not be able to sell your property!

Should I disclose the existence of black mold?

This is rapidly becoming the number one physical problem in selling real estate today. Buyers have heard horror stories about homes contaminated with black mold which supposedly gave the occupants terrible illnesses or caused their deaths. They've seen pest control people in oxygen masks and bubble suits go about attempting to remove the mold. The response has often been, "I don't want anything to do with a house that has black mold!" If yours does and you don't disclose it, it's almost an invitation for the buyers to come back at you later on. My suggestion is that if your home has black mold, you have it removed prior to putting it up for sale. You can still disclose the fact that mold was there and describe how it was removed. But, you also can tell buyers that your home is, for the moment, mold free. Keep in mind, however, that black mold grows almost everywhere there's moisture. My own guess is that the vast majority of homes have it somewhere in them. It's ubiquitous and most people probably live comfortably next to it, unaware that there's a problem. Indeed, as of this writing the Center for Disease Control (CDC) is studying the effects of black mold, but has not issued a definitive report on its toxic effects. Nevertheless, it's a bugaboo for buyers and it can kill a deal or force a significant price reduction. Therefore, find out if you have it, and get rid of it. (For your own safety, and to reassure buyers, use a licensed pest removal firm.)

Should I disclose heating/air problems?

Yes, if they exist. When I bought my current home, the sellers disclosed that the heater/air conditioner was the original system that came with the property, meaning it was 22 years old. They did not disclose, however, that it was broken. Indeed, it did work fine, for 5 years, until I had to have it replaced. You're not usually required to provide the buyers with a new heater/air conditioner, only one that works and that is safe. (If you're not sure about the safety of your system—for example, gas heaters can leak toxic gases into the home—have your local utility company check yours out. Or have a professional inspector look it over.) Only have a professional fix a gas problem.

Should I disclose electrical problems?

Yes, certainly. Electricity, as with gas, is nothing to fool around with. Someone could get seriously injured or even killed if there's a problem that's undisclosed. Ungrounded sockets or switches can be real problems as can plugs in bathrooms that don't have ground fault interrupter (GFI) circuits. If you have an electrical device that gives you a shock, unplug it or turn it off and have a professional look at it. While in theory it's probably enough to just tell the buyers about the problem, I prefer to have anything that involves a safety issue fixed prior to selling. That way I can sleep better at night. *Note:* If you're not sure, have a professional inspector check your home's electrical system. **Always be sure the power is off before doing any work on electrical systems.**

Should I disclose soil problems?

It depends on the nature of the problem. If you're selling a house with farmland that's so toxic you can't get anything to grow, then you've got a disclosable problem. On the other hand, if the soil tends to be rocky so it's hard (but not impossible) to dig down when planting tulips in your garden, then perhaps not. Shifting sands that can knock a home off its foundation, clay soil that tend to expand during the rainy season and buckle foundations, land that doesn't drain, or any other kind of soil problem that likely could affect the value of the property should, obviously, be disclosed.

Should I disclose zoning violations?

I would. It is possible to have a home for sale that's not in compliance with local zoning regulations. The easiest example is someone who's converted a garage to a small living area with bath and kitchen and then rents it out. Zoning probably demands only one house per lot, hence the conversion is not in compliance. If someone were purchasing the home with the intention of getting rental income from the garage conversion, he or she would likely be very unhappy to later discover that it was out of compliance, and worse, that the city demanded it be converted back. Yes, if you were the owner and disclosed the zoning violation, it undoubtedly would drop the value of your property, probably back to where it should be without the conversion. To pretend that a rental unit is legal only artificially raises the property's worth. *Note:* In my experience, while building departments will only rarely investigate nonpermitted work after the fact, planning departments are quick to look into zoning violations as soon as they are discovered, and to demand correction. All that it usually takes is for a neighbor to call up and complain.

Should I disclose problems with appliances?

You aren't normally obligated to provide a new appliance to a buyer. You don't even have to provide one that's spotless, although the buyer will undoubtedly complain if it's really dirty. However, the assumption is that the appliance will work, unless you disclose otherwise. Buyers will assume that the stove, oven, sink, garbage disposal, dishwasher, and other appliances work properly. If they don't, I would certainly disclose that fact. You also may want to let the buyer know if, even though an appliance does work, it has a significant problem.

Should I disclose a bad fireplace?

Yes, absolutely. Fireplaces are almost a given in homes with moderate to cold climates. That's not to say they are efficient at heating—most are not. But, they provide a certain ambiance that makes a home seem, well, homey. Most buyers consider a working fireplace to be an important part of the overall package. Therefore, if the fireplace doesn't work properly or is in some way broken, it significantly diminishes the value of the home in the buyer's eyes. If you sell a home without disclosing a bad fireplace, expect the buyers to be very angry at you when they discover the problem. However, beyond appearance, there's also a serious safety issue. A bad fireplace can leak toxic gases into a home with potentially dire consequences for the inhabitants. Or a bad fireplace can start a fire in the framing of the home resulting in its destruction. Sometimes a bad fireplace will drop loose bricks on the unwary inhabitant below, causing serious injury. All of which is to say that it's not something to play around with. If you suspect your fireplace has a problem, have it checked by a professional. If a problem is discovered, expect to either disclose that to the buyers, and discount the home price by the cost of fixing or replacing the fireplace. Or have it fixed or replaced yourself.

Should I disclose cracks, breaks, holes, and similar problems?

Cracks, holes, and breaks in walls, ceilings, floors, and foundations are not usually problems in and of themselves (unless they're fairly large). Rather, they are symptoms of what might be a more serious problem such as structural damage, a broken foundation, a bad roof, and so on. Therefore, even though they may be small, they could be significant. If you don't disclose them, a buyer can later say that he or she was unaware of the wall and floor cracks and, hence, had no idea the house needed a new foundation. Therefore, Mrs. or Mr. Seller, you can now pay for it. On the other hand, if you disclose the symptoms, even though you have no knowledge of whether they are serious or not, you can say to the buyer, "Hey, I pointed out the cracks, breaks, and holes to you. You went ahead and bought the property with full knowledge of them. So what are you complaining about?"

Should I disclose any homeowners' association problems?

Yes, this is very important. If your home is part of a condominium with a homeowners' association (HOA), or part of a co-op with a board of directors, there are certain potential liabilities you have. For example, if your HOA is sued (say someone fell and was injured on a common ownership street or an HOA employee hit a visitor), as a member, you could be responsible for payment of legal defense fees plus any damages if the organization lost the lawsuit. This could take the form of a sometimes sizeable assessment, extra money you'd have to pay each month. This is a danger that all HOAs face, hence, most are very careful, carry errors and omissions (E&O) and liability insurance, and do their level best to avoid such entanglements. In another common situation, the HOA might need to replace the roof of the building(s), but hasn't collected enough money in reserves. Each member could, again, be assessed. These are some of the problems associated with all community living and having an HOA. Buyers should be made aware of them by their agents and attorneys. However, where you come in is if you know of an existing lawsuit involving the HOA. Or, if you know of a coming assessment for some other problem, such as replacing a bad roof. You may even know of significant frictions among the homeowners themselves that have in the past, or could in the future, result in lawsuits. These are the sort of things to disclose to keep the buyers from later coming back and saying you sold the home under false pretenses.

Should I disclose any other problems or possible problems?

The general rule is, "When in doubt, better to be safe than sorry." When I sell a home I check many of the squares on the disclosure form that indicate possible problems. I disclose cracks in floors, ceilings, and walls, sometimes even when I haven't seen any! I point out that appliances could break, that plumbing and the roof could leak, and that a rotten tree could fall over. After all, I feel that the more I disclose, the less opportunity there is for the buyers to come back at me after the sale. Does it affect the price? Sometimes, but not usually, unless there's something serious, such as standing water in the basement, a bad roof, or a cracked foundation. However, you have to make your own decision on how much and what to disclose.

QUESTIONS TO ASK AN AGENT

Are there any mandatory state or federal disclosures I need to make? ☐

Your agent should make you aware of these. Many states have a specific form with specific statements on it that you must sign and give to buyers. The federal government also has mandatory disclosures with regard to lead. For lead there is a prescribed form you must use and a booklet you must give to the buyers. And with lead disclosures, buyers are allowed the opportunity to conduct an investigation and have 10 days after they receive the disclosure to go forward or bail out of the deal. In the future the federal government may mandate other disclosures, for example, regarding asbestos. A good real estate agent will key you into everything you need.

Will you make your own disclosures to the buyers? ☐

In some states, such as California, agents are required by law to conduct an evaluation of the property and disclose any defects they discover. Of necessity, these evaluations tend to be rather superficial and are couched in language such as "Does not appear to be damaged" or, "No problems observed." Nevertheless, it's a second opinion given to the buyers. A good agent will diligently go through your property and note any defects that he or she finds. The problem for you is if the agent discloses a defect that you don't. You can be sure the buyers are going to ask for verification. Therefore, I always show my disclosure sheet to the agent before presenting it to the buyers. This way, if there are any disagreements over what to disclose, they can be brought out into the open and discussed. Maybe the agent found some watermarks in the attic from an old leak long ago corrected that you thought were not worth noting, but which he or she says could indicate water leaking in. You can discuss with the agent whether or not you should *both* mention them. In other cases, you may want to ask the agent to change or remove some of the agent's disclosures. For example, once when I was selling a house an agent noted that the beams supporting the home had metal braces, suggesting the home wasn't structurally sound. When I pointed out that the so-called braces were actually earthquake retrofitting (a plus), the agent changed her report.

Will you assist me with my disclosures?

Agents may be hesitant to do this, lest you later say that they put words into your mouth, or told you what to say (or not say) that was other than what you believed. Agents have enough liability without having to worry about this. Hence, they are likely to limit the help they give you with disclosures. They may explain what disclosures are, give you some general rules on what should be disclosed, even show you how to fill out the form. But, it's unlikely they'll sit down and help you question by question. If an agent is willing to work closely with you in filling out the forms, it could be a real help. However, just be sure the agent doesn't, in fact, put words into your mouth. If you're worried about disclosing something and the agent says, "You don't have to bother with that," you may want to get a second opinion from your attorney.

Is there anything I should emphasize in my disclosures?

Sometimes simple statements of fact are all that are needed. For example, you could say that the posts of your fence are undermined by termites, the wood is rotten, and it's ready to fall over. Or, you might say that the fence posts have been weakened by termites. After all, the fence is still standing isn't it? Who is to say when or if it will collapse? You need to tell the buyers the nature of a problem, but you don't necessarily need to embellish it with all of the possibilities of what could happen in the future. Stick to the facts.

Is there anything I should fix immediately?

Your agent may give you a list. In theory, simply disclosing a problem to buyers should be enough. For example, you might say that the bathroom wall plug has shorted out and anyone taking a shower is likely to get electrocuted. You've put the buyer on notice. But, if you do nothing more, you could be guilty of selling a dangerous product. Therefore, whenever there are issues of health and safety, I have the problem corrected. (Chances are the buyers will demand you correct it anyhow.) This especially involves anything to do with electricity, gas, structural integrity, or other areas that could result in injury or worse if not fixed. A good agent will likely concur.

Should I get a professional home inspection first?

See what your agent thinks. If your home is fairly new
and seems to be in good shape, your agent will probably
tell you to wait until the buyers get it inspected. On the
other hand, if the agent suspects there's a problem, he or
she may suggest you will want to pay for your own professional inspection to ferret it out. Sometimes agents can
spot things that we, as homeowners, have gotten used to
living with and are oblivious to.

Is there anything I need not disclose?

This is tricky. Most agents will tell you to disclose anything significant to the buyers. But, who's to say what's
significant or not? If you aren't sure, ask your agent. He
or she should want to protect you, as much as him- or
herself. But always take their advice with a grain of salt.
Remember, the agent doesn't get paid a commission until
the home is sold. And if the agent fears that disclosing
something might lose the deal, there's always the chance
he or she might say, "Oh, don't mention it to the buyers…
what they don't know won't hurt them." Maybe that's
true, but it could come back to wallop you. Use your own
judgment (or that of your attorney) as the final arbiter.

Is there anything I should hide from the buyers?

Of course, a good agent will simply say, "No, get it all out
on the table." But, what if your agent should say something such as, "Well, now that you mention it, it wouldn't
hurt to patch that crack in the basement wall and paint
over it so the buyers don't see it." As noted above, failure
to disclose can come back to bite you. But going out of
your way to hide or disguise a defect can be worse.

6
Handling the Buyer's Home Inspection

QUESTIONS TO ASK YOURSELF

Should I allow the buyer to have an inspection?

If you don't, chances are you won't have a buyer for long. In today's real estate market, professional home inspections by buyers almost go without saying. In one way or another, they are a part of virtually every real estate contract. The buyers want to know, and rightly so, if there are undisclosed defects in the home you are selling. One way they can find out is to have a professional inspector check out the property. Besides, the inspection report can actually help protect you. If after the sale the buyers come back with a complaint about an undisclosed defect, you can always tell them they hired their own professional inspector to check out the house. If he or she didn't find the problem, how could you be expected to know about it? Of course, a lot depends on what the problem is, whether it was concealed from the buyers and inspector, and a whole raft of other considerations. Nevertheless, by allowing the buyers unrestricted access to professionally inspect your home, you show them you have nothing to hide and you help build a case that there's no hidden defects.

How much time should I give the buyers?

The problem with a home inspection is that it can be used as a device to allow the buyer to avoid committing to the deal. Most sellers think their home is sold once the buyers have signed off on the sales agreement. But, that's naïve. Actually, the deal isn't locked up until the buyers have signed off on all the contingencies. (And it isn't for sure until title transfers and you get your money!) One of the most common contingencies is that the buyers must approve a professional inspection report. Until they approve that report, the deal is as fragile as thin ice. If they have 3 weeks to approve the report, then you won't know if your deal is firmed up for 3 weeks. Therefore, it's usually to a seller's advantage to keep the period for the home inspection as short as possible. The less time for the buyers to approve, the shorter the time your house is in limbo and, in many cases, off the market. On the other hand, with the volume of sales in recent years, it can take a week or two to line up an inspector. Therefore, common practice has dictated that the time for a professional inspection is typically 2 weeks. That should give the buyers enough time to conduct most inspections and to check out the reports. Of course, some buyers request longer, but if they do, I would suspect they may not want to commit to the deal. *Note:* If the initial inspection finds a problem, say something involving standing water, the buyers may demand additional time for a more technical report, for example, from a soils engineer. You don't have to give the extra time, but you might as well, since without it, the buyers are likely to walk… and with it, they may just go ahead and purchase the house.

Should I require a copy of the report?

Yes, you should. This should be part of your contingency upon allowing the professional inspection. The buyers can do the inspection, within a specified timeframe, provided they give you a copy of the report and allow you to show that copy to any future buyers of the home. The reason this is important is first, you want to see what the report says. After all, if the buyers say the report says you need a new roof and you don't have a copy, how do you know what they are saying is accurate? Second, if the buyers don't go through with the purchase and you put your home back on the market, a future buyer will likely demand to see all previous home inspection reports. If you don't have a copy that you are allowed to show, you could be in a very difficult position. *Note:* Some inspection reports state quite clearly on them that they are to be shown only to the person who orders the report and to whomever else that person allows to see it. That's why you want to be sure you have permission to show the report to future buyers.

Should I pay for the inspection?

You may be asked to pay for the inspection, although in most cases, it's the one who orders the report (the buyer) who is responsible for paying for it. Of course, as with everything else in real estate, it's a matter of negotiation and common practice. The buyer wants the report and wants you to pay the cost. Do you? You might, if you're desperate to sell. Or you might simply insist that the buyers are to pay for their own professional inspection report. Of course, that may constitute a rejection of their offer and they might walk. Or, they simply might have been testing to see how much they could get away with, and they'll agree. Keep in mind that it's common practice for the buyers to pay for their own professional inspection report. On the other hand, it's equally common practice for the sellers to pay for a termite inspection and any repair work necessary to get a termite clearance. (The termite clearance is a common requirement that lenders make before they will fund loans to buyers.)

Should I go along with the inspector?

I would, but a lot depends on your physical capabilities. Inspectors not only wander through the house, but typically go up into the attic, in the basement, and in the crawlspace under the house. It can be dirty and dangerous. (You could step wrong in the attic and fall through the thin sheetrock ceiling into the room below—don't laugh, I've seen it happen!) Do you feel comfortable going such places? If not, then stay away. But if you do, you can learn a lot. While you can expect the written report to note any defects found, going along with the inspector can help clarify the problem to you. And the inspector often can suggest remedies, both inexpensive and costly. Finally, sometimes the inspector will mistake something and you can make a correction. For example, you and the inspector may be up in the attic and he or she spots watermarks on some of the rafters. "Aha," the inspector says, "You've got a leaky roof." "Had," you reply. "We had it fixed last year. Hasn't leaked since."

"Oh," says the inspector and makes a note. Now the written report, instead of saying something about likely leaks in the roof, will probably say that watermarks indicate past leaks, which the owner notes have been fixed. It can make a big difference when the buyer reads the report. By the way, you also can expect the buyer to go along with the inspection, for the same reasons you are there! You can be a threesome learning as you go.

Should I agree to fix the problems?

Maybe… and maybe not. Often a professional inspection report will list a series of defects in the property. For example, there might be mold growing on the bathroom floor as a result of water splashed from a shower. A wall plug in the living room might be inoperative or sparking. A portion of a fence might be falling down, and so on. Of course, there could be more serious problems as well. For example, the report may indicate your roof has worn out and needs to be replaced. As soon as you get the report, should you go out and fix things? If there's something involving health and safety, for example, a broken electrical plug, then I would have it fixed at once. (Have it done professionally to avoid liability issues.) After all, whoever's living in the house may be at risk and that could include you and your family. On the other hand, as for the other defects noted, I would wait for the buyer to make a demand. Typically, soon after receiving the report they will send a notice that they will approve it *providing* the following items are fixed. What they are saying is that their purchase now hinges on your making the corrections. To save the sale, you may want to go ahead and do the fixes. This is usually the case if they are minor and inexpensive. On the other hand, if we're talking about fixes at the level of a roof, which can easily cost $10,000 to $20,000 to replace, it's probably negotiation time. You may offer to fix, but not replace the roof. The buyers may counter that they want a new roof. You may counter that since they will get the benefit of a new roof, they should pay at least half the cost. And so on. It's like going through the selling process all over again. But don't get discouraged. Most buyers still want the house and will bend to get it, including sometimes paying for at least some of the fixes.

Should I renegotiate the price?

This is an alternative when the professional inspection report comes in with problems. The report says the house needs a new roof and the buyers demand you replace it. You counter offer to take $7000 off the price and then they can go out and get their own new roof. This has certain advantages to buyers, particularly if they are cash short. Your credit can be toward their closing costs, helping them to get into the house. And later they can get a roof of their choosing, not yours. Further, with a cash settlement there won't be a time lapse while a contractor is found and the work completed. On the other hand, buyers (and sometimes lenders) will insist the actual work be done and no cash compromise may be possible. Further, sometimes difficult buyers will use a problem found in the inspection report as a wedge to get a much more significant price reduction from you. For example, they may point to some cracks noted at the periphery of the house and say that it indicates a new foundation is needed. They figure the cost to be $50,000 and they want you to reduce the price by that amount. Do cracks indicate a broken foundation? Maybe. Will it cost $50,000 to fix? Maybe. Or perhaps they'll take your money and then just live in the house as it is. You have to decide whether you're so desperate to sell that you're willing to cut the price, or whether you'll simply cut loose the buyers and hope that some future buyers will be more reasonable. By the way, you will most likely have to show the old buyers' professional inspection report to new buyers.

Do I have to produce earlier inspection reports?

Often you are asked for them. A buyer's inspection contingency will typically not only ask for a professional inspection and report, but also will ask you to turn over all previous inspection reports. If you had one just a month earlier, it's going to be hard to say you forgot about it or lost it. Thus, the next potential buyer is going to see whatever problems the last buyer who ordered a report found. All of which is to say, found problems tend not to go away. They must usually be dealt with either by fixing them or with a cash solution.

Should I give the buyer an allowance?

Sometimes you're aware of a problem with the house. For example, a frequent problem in some areas of the country are plumbing pipes. Put in 30 years or so ago, they are made of galvanized iron, which tends to rust over time. Now, 30 years later, leaks pop up all over the place. While any individual leak can be fixed, the whole plumbing system needs to be replaced with copper, which should cure the problem. However, it will cost $10,000 for the fix and you don't want to spend the money. One alternative is to disclose the problem directly to the buyers before they make the inspection (and uncover it for themselves) and offer a lump sum, say $2500 toward fixing the problem. You can point out that this isn't enough for a complete fix, but it is likely enough to fix leaks as they occur for a long time. And if the buyers choose, they can apply the money toward a complete and more expensive fix. By getting the problem out in the open early and by offering a solution, you preempt the buyers' "discovery" of it and demand for it being fixed. Of course, there's nothing to keep the buyers from saying they want the entire house replumbed by you. But, you can point out, for example, that you've only lived there 9 years and they are moving in and might stay there for another 9 years. Why should it be your entire responsibility to pay for the fix? No, giving an allowance won't work every time, but sometimes it will work. And when it does, it might just save you a few bucks.

Can I save money by doing corrective work myself?

Yes... and no. It depends on how much you value your labor... and how good a job you can do. If you figure you'll fix the problem over a few weekends in your spare time, then you might indeed be able to save some money. Calling in a plumber can easily cost $60 an hour or more. If it's a 6-hour job, you can save $360 if you do it yourself, even if it takes you 10 hours to complete. However, the other side of the bargain is how well it comes out. If, for example, your home needs a new water heater and you figure you'll save the installation charge by doing it yourself, you better end up with a water heater that's snugly in place (including tie-downs to ensure it doesn't fall over in earthquakes or windstorms), with fittings that don't leak, and with safety values and drains correctly in place. Oh, and you'll also need a building permit. Does having it done professionally suddenly seem more appealing? My own rule of thumb is that I'll have it done professionally if the work meets any one of three criteria:

- There's a safety and health issued involved, such as gas or electricity.
- It needs to come out looking great, such as plastering.
- It must be done quickly and I don't have the time or inclination to do it.

On the other hand, if the work doesn't fall into any of the above categories, I will sometimes do it myself.

Should I pay for a termite inspection?

Here's how it works: In nearly all areas of the country, in order for the buyer to get financing, the lender requires a termite clearance. This is a special form usually from a licensed inspector stating the home is free from termites and certain other pests. No clearance, no buyer's loan. No buyer's loan, no sale. Hence, you need to get the clearance, which by itself only costs a few dollars. However, to get the clearance, you need to have your home inspected by a licensed termite pest inspector, which often can cost several hundred dollars. Hence, in most areas, the sellers pay for the inspection and the clearance. If that's all you're asked to pay for, I would go ahead and do so, and consider myself lucky. Of course, you can refuse to pay and instead insist that the buyers pay for the inspection and clearance. And they just might, if they want the house and it's a seller's market. However, that probably would be a rare instance.

Should I pay for corrective termite work?

If termites or certain other pests are found, the inspector won't issue the clearance until they are removed and damaged wood replaced. The fix can cost just a few hundred dollars when it might simply involve replacing some infected timbers. Or it might cost thousands of dollars if, for example, the entire house must be tented and fumigated. Just remember, without the termite clearance, chances are your buyer won't be able to get financing and probably won't be able to make the purchase even if he or she wants to. Therefore, you probably will have to pay for the corrective work. However, there's another category that involves preventive work. Normally this is up to the buyers. If they want certain work done, hopefully, to prevent the return of termites, it's usually their prerogative. You normally don't need to pay for any preventive work (and lenders normally don't require that it be done).

Can I refuse to sell if the termite repair work is too costly?

That depends on what you signed in the sales (and the listing) agreement. Very often these agreements are open-ended. They say something to the effect that while the buyers are responsible for preventive work, the sellers agree to pay for all corrective work caused by termites and certain other pests. The assumption is that even if termites are found, it won't cost too much to have the work done. But what if, in your worst nightmare, it turns out the house is completely infected and ready to fall down? The inspection report says the entire structure needs to be replaced, at a cost of $100,000! Are you required to pay this? You could technically be on the hook for it, depending on what your sales contract says. However, as a practical matter it's more likely the buyers will gracefully back out and you'll be stuck with a falling down house. However, for smaller amounts (and even for a huge amount), the buyers could insist you pay for the fix since you agreed upon it. To avoid this problem when I sell an older home that's likely to have termites, I often include a maximum price I'll pay for repair work, say $3000 in both the listing and sales agreements. If the amount is higher, then I can make the decision to do the work, or not sell. While this gives me a doorway out, it also presents problems in convincing buyers to go ahead in making an offer, since they tend to immediately assume that

I know there's a big problem with termites, something which may not be true.

Can I demand a different inspection report?

Yes, you can. You can call in and pay for your own inspector. The new report may confirm what the earlier report says, or it may dispute it. And it's often up to the buyers to decide which opinion to accept. If an inspection report finds something wrong with my house and I know, or suspect, that the problem isn't real, I'll not hesitate to get another opinion. For example, once when selling a house an inspector said the roof was leaking because there were water marks on the wall of one bedroom. I knew those marks were caused not by a leaking roof, but by a water pipe which had leaked (and was since fixed) in an adjoining bathroom. I called in another inspector who confirmed this. The fix was not to replace the roof, but to repaint the wall. It makes a big difference. However, keep in mind that buyers can be fickle. While you're running around trying to get another inspection, they may simply disapprove of their inspection and back out of the purchase. Sometimes it's better to deal with what's found, even if inaccurate, than to try and get a whole new inspection.

Can I demand a different person do the work?

Yes, if the buyer goes along with it. A common example is when the buyer calls in a roofer to inspect the roof. The roofer, who also happens to be a contractor, says it needs to be replaced at a cost of $18,000. Now the buyer wants you to pay for it. However, you figure it should only cost half that amount. So, you call in your own roofer, who says the job can be done for $9000. You tell the buyers you'll fix the roof, but you'll choose the contractor. The buyers may try to insist that their contractor do the work, but unless they can come up with a convincing argument showing why and how he or she will do a better job ($9000 worth), you'll probably end up having your worker do the work. Always be wary of any work involving construction where there's only one bid. You should always try to get at least three bids to be sure that you're not getting cheated.

QUESTIONS TO ASK AN AGENT

Do you recommend a particular inspector?

If you decide that you want to call for your own inspection, who better to recommend an inspector than a real estate agent who, presumably, works with them day in and day out? Expect your agent to say something such as, "Yes, why don't you call Joe. He's done a lot of good work for me over the years." However, before you call Joe keep in mind that what a real estate agent may call good work and what you want could possibly be two different things. An agent may like an inspector who rarely finds problems and, hence, facilitates sales. You, on the other hand, may want a detailed inspection to uncover any problems so you can correct them before a sale and before a buyer's inspector locates them. This is not to say you should discount an agent's recommendation, you shouldn't. It's just to note that the recommendation should be taken with a grain of salt.

Should I do the corrective work or pay a professional?

Your agent often can give you good advice here and steer you away from an expensive mistake. Too often we're inclined to do the work ourselves, particularly if we're at all handy. Your agent, on the other hand, may point out the difficulties of the task, the short timeframe involved, and the need to come up with a professional looking result. In short, most of the time expect your agent to suggest work be done by a professional...but not always. Sometimes the agent will understand your desire to save money by doing it yourself, will know of your capabilities because of previous work you've done, and may realize that the work will not involve health and safety issues nor will be readily visible (such as in the attic or under the house) to buyers. Hence, a good agent will make an honest recommendation for doing it yourself or for hiring a professional. Listen to what your agent says.

Should I renegotiate the price?

Again, your agent can help you decide between paying for the fix or offering (or accepting) a lower price. Presumably your agent has had years of experience in this and can tell you which direction is most likely to produce better results. Also, agents often will know which work must be done to satisfy lenders' demands and which can be handled by a discount.

Will you handle negotiations?

This should go without saying, nevertheless, you want to be clear on it. If the buyers are demanding a pricey fix, will your agent try to negotiate a less costly approach or a price discount, or is this something you will need to handle yourself? Any good agent should do this for you, if for no other reason than to save the deal. But, I have seen agents who, once the purchase contract has been signed, disappear and suddenly you're on your own. I don't know whether they are simply too busy, are afraid of liability issues, or don't know the answers. But such behavior is certainly unprofessional. Hopefully, your agent will stand by your side through thick and thin. Unfortunately, if your agent doesn't, you'll have to pick up the pieces and do the negotiating yourself, as it's usually too late to find another agent once the purchase contract is signed.

Are the corrections demanded reasonable?

This is particularly a problem with demands for big concessions. For example, the buyers disapprove of the inspection report and insist they'll only go forward with the purchase if you cut the price $75,000. It's important to get practical input here. Are the demands reasonable? Or are the buyers simply unrealistic? Or are they trying to force a major price concession out of you? A good agent can tell you which is the case and you can then act accordingly. (If it's reasonable, your agent may suggest you discount the home or do the work. If it's unrealistic, the agent will probably want you to counter. And if it's a ploy to drive your price way down, the agent may actually suggest you walk from the deal!)

Are there alternatives?

There are always alternatives. A good agent can find these for you. He or she may suggest getting a new report (although I've found agents hesitant to recommend this), or may know of a cheaper contractor, or may suggest negotiating for a less costly discount, or whatever. A good agent will always be on your side, always looking for ways not only to complete the deal but to be sure that you get the most you can out of it. Therefore, never hesitate to ask for alternatives.

7

The Challenge: Counteroffers

QUESTIONS TO ASK YOURSELF

Should I accept the buyer's offer?

☐

That's the really big question. You've fixed up your home. You've found an agent and listed it. And now, here's a buyer offering to purchase it. Should you accept? If the offer is for less than you're asking or for lesser terms (paper instead of cash), you may want to reject the offer. But if it's the best offer you're likely to get, you may still want to accept… or at least counter. On the other hand, if it's for the full asking price, you'll certainly feel like accepting. Or, if the market's very hot and you think even better offers may come in—you may want to reject higher than the asking price! (Beware, depending on how your listing agreement reads, rejecting a full price offer can trigger a requirement that you pay the agent a commission anyway! See Chapter 4.) If the offer is for more than asking price, you have to ask yourself, are there other, still better offers coming in? Making any decision requires that you understand the offer, the market, and yourself.

Do I understand the buyer's offer?

☐

It's not usually as simple as, "I'll offer $300,000, cash." The offer itself is presented in written form, typically in a document referred to by many names (sales/purchase agreement, deposit receipt, contract offer, and so on). This document is often pages long containing a lot of fine print or boilerplate material. In fact, some offers seem to be nothing more than a dozen pages of boilerplate with very little written in by hand. The reason for this is that the offer is intended to be a legally binding document. Hence, it needs to have concise language and not contain loopholes through which either buyer or seller can escape. Typically, the boilerplate is important so it's written by the agent's or the real estate board's attorneys. Usually the agent only fills in such things as the address of the property, the price, the amount of the deposit, and the amount financed. All other areas are already written out in the document and all the agent does to make them apply is check an appropriate box. All of which is to say that while it can seem confusing at first, after you've read through it once or twice you should be able to make sense of it. Your agent can help here. Remember, don't just look at the price. Look at all the other conditions including financing, downpayment, deposit, time of occupancy, and contingencies. If there's anything you don't understand, ask your agent. Also, check with your attorney. Once you sign, you may be bound by the terms of the agreement.

Are there contingencies in the buyer's offer?

A contingency in an offer is when the buyer says the purchase is "subject to" something happening (or not happening). For example, a common contingency is that the purchase is subject to the buyer being able to obtain needed financing. If the buyer doesn't qualify for the mortgage, the deal's off. (Which is why it's a good idea to ask for a letter of preapproval by a lender from the buyer, just so you'll know you've got a "live one.") Most offers contain contingencies that protect the buyer. The most common contingencies are:

- Financing contingency (buyer must obtain needed financing for the deal to go through),
- Professional home inspection contingency (buyer must approve a home inspection report),
- Termite clearance (seller must provide a termite clearance),

- Disclosure contingency (buyer must approve seller's disclosures), and

- Other contingencies specific to this deal such as the buyer being able to sell his or her current home.

The more contingencies in the offer, normally the weaker it is. The reason is simply that there are more ways for the buyer to get out of the deal. In fact, much of the escrow process involves removing the buyer's contingencies until the sale actually goes through.

Are the contingencies frivolous or reasonable?

This is something you must decide. Normally the contingencies noted above are considered reasonable. In other words, no prudent buyer would make an offer without them. However, in a very hot market, to beat out other bidders, a buyer may make a "noncontingent" offer, one without any contingencies—here, presumably, if the buyer can't perform, the deposit is almost surely forfeited… and you may have the option to sue for damages. However, there can be unreasonable contingencies. As a wild example, the offer could be contingent upon a tidal wave hitting the East coast of the United States. This is obviously frivolous and an offer no seller is likely to seriously consider. On the other hand, frivolous contingencies may be less obvious. The buyer is planning on getting money from Aunt Helen to make the purchase, hence, it's subject to Aunt Helen approving of the house. Not entirely unreasonable. Except that there's no real deal here until Aunt Helen gets herself down and looks at the property.

Can I limit the buyer's contingencies?

Yes, and you may want to. However, remember that anytime you make a change to the offer, you've rejected it. (See below.) To take our above example, you may limit the Aunt Helen contingency by giving the buyer 3 days to get her approval. If she approves within 3 days, it's a deal. If the buyer can't get her to go for it by then, there's no deal. It may be worth your while to tie up your property for a few days in the hopes that a deal can be made. In a broader scope, almost any contingency can be limited by time and/or performance. For example, you may have to give the buyer time to conduct a professional home inspection. But not unlimited time. Typically this contingency is limited to 14 days (although any amount can be agreed upon). You may limit a buyer's financing contingency by allowing, say, 3 weeks, to come up with a letter of commitment from a lender, else the deal is off. Limiting the buyer's contingencies is one way of protecting yourself.

Can I accept and still change the buyer's offer?

Oh, if only this were possible! Consider, the buyer makes an offer of $310,000 for your property. The only change you make is to up the amount to $320,000. A paltry $10,000 more and it's a done deal—so easy, so wonderful! But, no buyer would accept such an outrageous change. In fact, buyers won't accept *any* change, no matter how small. For example, they want an escrow to run for 3 weeks, you change it to 4 weeks. A minor thing because you need more time to get out. But, you've effectively rejected their offer. Unless they agree to your change, there's no deal. And they have the option of agreeing or not. The rule is that you can only accept the buyer's offer *exactly* as presented. Change anything and you have, in effect, made a counteroffer. Of course, in practice, small changes seldom cause a deal to be scuttled. The buyer wants to include the refrigerator. You want to take it with you. So you cross out the part about the refrigerator on the sale agreement and send it back to the buyer, confident he or she will sign. But in the meantime, the buyer has found another house. He or she is delighted that you've countered, because it gives the buyer an opportunity to walk away from the deal without losing a deposit or having other entanglements. Your small change cost you the deal. It's something to think about the next time you decide you don't want to accept the buyer's offer exactly as presented.

Should I make a counteroffer?

It's risky, for reasons noted above. My suggestion is that you try very hard to accept the buyer's offer as it is presented. Only if you can't live with it, should you then consider a counter. A counteroffer is like a brand new offer, only this time you're making it to the buyer, instead of the other way around. To make it more palatable to the buyer, your agent may use the same document on which the buyer's offer was made, just writing in the changes and having you initial them. If the buyer agrees with the changes, in writing, the deal can be made. However, no matter on what document it's written, the buyer has the option of turning down your counter. In which case there's no deal. Of course, the buyer can counter back, sometimes on the same document, hoping to make a counteroffer more palatable to you! This can go back and forth many times until there is acceptance all around... or not.

Should I counter on price?

This is what most buyers... and sellers, are hung up on. Everyone wants their price. You want yours. But to get yours, the buyer may not be able to get his or hers. Of course, a lot will depend on market conditions. If you're in a seller's market where there are oodles of buyers competing to find homes, you can pretty much demand and get your price. But, if it happens to be a buyer's market with oodles of sellers competing for a few buyers, it's more likely they will prevail in a contest over price. One alternative to consider is giving the buyer his or her price (or close to it) and demand tighter terms. For example, you may need to stay in your home for an additional 5 months until the kids are out of school. So you give the buyer his or her price, but insist you keep possession for 5 months. This is a very demanding concession and important to you, else you'll have to rent a place for 5 months. The buyer won't get the property for nearly half a year. If you find you need more time at the end of the 5 months, and the buyer is adamant about you vacating at the originally established time, you have some leeway. Since you'll have the rights of a tenant, the buyer can't just ask you to leave. He or she might have to go to court and get an unlawful detainer action (eviction) to get you out. But, the buyer is getting his or her price. It's all a matter of negotiation.

Should I counter on terms?

The buyer offers to put 20 percent down and get an 80 percent mortgage at 6 percent interest. But, you're apart $10,000 on price. However, you're retiring, you own the home free and clear, and you need income from the money you'll get. If you put the money from the sale in the bank, you'll be lucky to get 2 percent at current rates. However, you counter the buyer by saying you'll accept the price, providing the buyer gives you a first mortgage at 8 percent interest. If the house is selling for $300,000, that means that instead of getting $240,000, which you'll bank at 2 percent, you'll lend it to the buyer at 8 percent, a difference of $400 a month versus $1600 a month. It's only 2 percent more to the buyer, who is getting his or her price, but it's a huge monthly difference to you. Depending on your situation, countering on terms can be a highly creative and productive way of making a deal work to your advantage.

Should I counter the contingencies?

It depends. Accept them if you can. But, if you can't live with them, then by all means counter. For example, the buyers may want a finance contingency that gives them 60 days to get financing on your property. Sixty days in our age of electronic mortgages sounds unreasonable. Even during times when financing is peaking and lenders are overloaded, most manage to get the job done in 3 weeks, 4 at most. Therefore, you may feel that the buyers' asking for 60 days means they are having trouble getting financing. So, for example, you may want to counter the contingency by saying they must provide you with a letter of commitment from a lender in no more than 21 days. In other words, the lender is ready, willing, and able to fund the loan at that time. Or, you may change the 60 days to 30 days. Remember, you have to ask yourself why does a buyer want a particular contingency. As another example, buyers may insist on a home sale contingency. They'll go through with the purchase of your home, but only providing they can sell their home first. Until they sell their home, they won't go through with the purchase of yours. If the market is slow, you may be tempted to agree. However, you might counter the contingency by saying that you will continue to keep your house on the market and should you get another offer from a different buyer, you will give the first buyers 72 hours to remove their contingency. In other words, you're giving them first refusal should another offer appear. If the buyers have another house to sell first, they very well might agree to this.

What if the buyers accept my counter?

Put the champagne in the refrigerator. (But don't drink it until escrow closes and you get your money!) The deal's on the way to completion. Just be sure you tie up all the details. For example, if there were counters and counter-counters, be sure you get a written copy of the final accepted offer with the buyers' signatures on it. The agent calling to tell you they've accepted is terrific. But in real estate, the Statute of Frauds says that everything must be in writing to be enforceable, so insist on getting that signed document as soon as possible. Next, you or your agent should open an escrow that will accept the buyers' downpayment, their deposit, and funds from a lender, and that will hold a deed you sign to them. This can take a few weeks and in the interim all the buyers' contingencies will need to be removed and any problems you have with title to your property discovered and cleared. Getting the buyers to accept is a big step, but don't start celebrating just yet.

What if they reject it?

There's nothing to keep the buyers from walking away from your counteroffer (any more than there is to keep you from rejecting their initial or counteroffers). It's a risk you take when you counter. I've been asked what the percentages are here. How often will the buyers actually reject a seller's counteroffer—10 percent of the time? 25 percent? 80 percent? The truth is there are no percentages. Every offer, seller, and buyer are different. It's a brand new horse race every time, and you can never know what the buyers will do. Of course, if they reject your counter, then you can try what I call a "desperation counter." You can come back accepting the last offer they made, which is now in the form of a new counteroffer by you. Will they take it? Maybe. I've seen it happen. But now you're accepting an offer you initially rejected. And they've seen how weak a bargaining position you have. They may reject your desperation counter and make an even lower offer!

Should I "split the difference"?

This is a trap that sellers sometimes get into. You're asking $300,000 for your home. The buyer's offer is $280,000. Your bottom price is $290,000 so you agree to split the difference. You counter at your $290,000 bottom, figuring that will make the deal. But the buyer, seeing that you've come down $10,000, figures you'll come down more. So now he or she splits the difference and offers $285,000. Suddenly splitting the difference has driven you below your bottom price. Beware of this tactic even if suggested by an agent. The only time it really works is if it's clear to both buyer and seller that splitting the difference is as low as you go. In other words, sometimes agents will get together and speak to both buyers and sellers saying something like, "We're some distance apart in price. Will you agree to split the difference?" If the buyer agrees and you agree, then it's just a matter of writing it down and signing. Just remember, until it's signed and delivered, it's no deal.

Should I walk away?

There are probably only two times you should walk away. The first is when the deal is a real stinker and you don't want any part of it. Then you should run, not walk! The other time is when you do it for effect. Walking away can be a very effective negotiating tool, if done correctly. The easiest example to see is when buying a car. You may be arguing with the dealer over the price. The dealer won't budge. So, instead of accepting the dealer's last offer, you walk out of the showroom. Chances are before you get off the lot, a salesperson will haul you back in with a better deal. Similarly, in real estate you may have negotiated with the buyer for some time and simply can't come to an agreement on terms or price. Finally, you say, in effect, take my last offer or forget it. You simply walk away from the negotiations. At this point, if the buyer is not really interested in the property he or she, too, will walk and the negotiations will be unsuccessful. But at least you'll sense that no deal to your satisfaction could have been made. On the other hand, if the buyer really does want the property, he or she may just say, "Hold up! I'll take it," and accepts your last offer. It's sort of like betting the whole thing on one throw of the dice.

Do I know how to accept an offer?

These days with a strong market and sometimes multiple offers, agents often just FAX them in. However, you can at least expect your own agent to come to you with the offer and to explain it. Listen carefully to the entire offer. Don't simply hear the price and turn it off. There just might be terms that will interest you. Your agent should go over it carefully point by point. If there's something you don't understand, be sure to ask for clarification. If you still don't understand, stop. Check with your attorney. Don't go forward not understanding the ramifications of what you're signing. Remember, you haven't accepted the offer until your signature is on the line.

How long should I give the buyers to accept my counter?

Normally a counteroffer (or any offer for that matter) is accompanied by a time limit. You can give the buyers a week to accept your counter. Or a day. Or an hour. It's up to you. My own preference is to give them as little time as possible. This forces them to make a decision, even if it's not to buy. It also helps keep them from spotting another property they might like better than yours in the interim! If the buyers are readily available, then usually I give them only a few hours, say until 12 midnight. Or perhaps until noon the next day to accept. After all, they've seen the house. They've established that they want to buy it by their initial offer. Now you're only negotiating price and terms. A short fuse here often works to your advantage.

QUESTIONS TO ASK AN AGENT

How will you let me know when I receive an offer?

Most times it's obvious. The agent will call and come over with the offer. But you might be planning to go out of town. Or the agent might. Or you are on the road a lot and can only be reached on your cell phone. Or... there are any number of reasons why hooking up with the agent can be difficult. Yet, you want to get that offer as soon as it's made. After all, you don't want the buyers to get antsy and start looking at other homes. You want to strike while the iron's hot, get them while they're still anxious to buy (and, hopefully, pay the most). Therefore, it behooves you to ask the agent how he or she will let you know there's an offer and how it will be presented to you. Setting this up in advance can avoid wasted effort and a lot of unnecessary scurrying around later on.

Will you present other offers as received?

It's important that you get this straight with your agent. You want *all* offers presented to you as they are received. What you don't want is your agent to sit on an offer while waiting for you to decide on an earlier one. Both ethics and real estate law normally require that an agent do this. However, sometimes agents forget or are a bit lax, particularly if the first offer happens to be from them or their office. Make it perfectly clear that you want to see every offer immediately. After all, you might be considering an offer of $250,000 for your property while another for $275,000 is waiting in the wings. As soon as the second shows up, you're very likely to forget about the first.

Will the buyer's agent, or you, or both present the offer?

Traditionally in real estate, once an offer comes in, the buyer's agent will call the seller's agent letting him or her know. Your agent will call you and arrange a time for the presentation. Then both the buyer's agent and your agent will show up and present the offer. Often the buyer's agent will make the presentation with your agent making clarifications or stepping in if something is presented which is not satisfactory. However, this nice and neat method has been turned on its head by the hot real estate market early in this century. Often there are multiple offers on a property. This could result in multiple buyers' agents pounding on your door wanting to present their offers. It could become quite chaotic. Therefore, today buyers' agents will often just FAX their offer in to your agent, who should come out with it and other offers that have come in to give you a chance to accept, reject, or counter them. Further, if offers are flying in, your agent may suggest simply waiting a day or two to decide until more have come in and buyers have bid up the price. (One buyer isn't supposed to know what another is bidding, but somehow word often seems to get out.) Then your agent may come over and go through all of them with you. (No, this is not the same as holding them back from you, discussed above. It's only suggesting that you hold off making a decision until more and perhaps better offers are in. It's still up to you. Of course, anytime you wait, you give the buyers a chance to fly the coup.)

Can you explain everything I don't understand?

Of course your agent can. After all, that's part of what he or she is getting paid to do. However, sometimes a strange offer will come in that even your agent can't fathom. At that point, it would be wise to get the buyer's agent (assuming he or she isn't already present) to present it and make clear the offer. If you still don't understand, then get your attorney to check it out. Never accept, reject, or counter an offer that you don't fully understand.

What constitutes a good offer?

If the agent truly thinks it's a good offer, he or she should be able to explain why. This will be obvious if it's for cash and full price. However, in a very hot market you may want to ask about bidders pushing up beyond the asking price. On the other hand, if the offer is for less than you are asking and your agent wants you to accept, you should ask for an explanation. For example, your agent may tell you that the reason you haven't had any previous or higher offers is that your house isn't in the best of shape, or you have it priced too high. He or she may point out market conditions, which might be slow. And so on. What's important to get is not just the opinion, but the explanation. Then you can judge for yourself whether your agent is right and whether you should accept the offer. Keep in mind, however, that agents don't usually get paid unless and until you accept an offer, so there's always a impetus on the part of the agent to get you to sign. Nevertheless, a good agent should always put your interests first, and that means getting the best offer possible.

Why is it a bad offer?

Sometimes your agent will indicate he or she doesn't think much of the offer. It's an opinion. Your question should be why. Perhaps the agent will say that he or she has heard there are other, better offers coming in soon. In talking with other agents, perhaps another one or two or even three offers may be on the way by morning or the next day. Why accept a low offer when a better one may be forthcoming? The question now becomes, is one in the hand worth two in the bush? I've had agents call saying they were in the process of writing up an offer that would be presented within the hour. After 3 hours pass, I call back. The agent expresses regret that at the last minute the buyers changed their minds. You need to consider the offer you have, not the offer you might get. Or your agent may say the offer is simply too low, your house is worth more given market conditions. Or the terms are onerous. Now it's a judgment call. You have the agent's opinion and explanation… now you decide.

Should I accept?

Good agents are loath to tell their sellers to accept any offer. They don't want the burden to be placed on them if it later turns out that a better offer was just around the corner. They don't want to make the big decision that's really only the seller's to make. On the other hand, sometimes as a seller you need a kind of "Dutch Uncle" guidance. You need someone to finally say, "Go ahead and do it!" It's usually best if your agent is reluctant to tell you to accept an offer, but only does so after you pester them about what to do. An agent who is too eager to tell you to accept (or reject, for that matter) an offer may simply want to get the deal done and move on to the next one. Such an agent may not have your best interests at heart.

If I don't accept, what should I counter on?

Here a good agent's advice can be invaluable. Chances are the agent has had a chance to sound out the buyers, or at least the buyers' agent. Your agent may have a sense of how much more they may be willing to pay or what terms they might agree to. Listen to what your agent says. However, be sure that you're listening to *your* agent, that he or she has agreed to be a seller's agent. You want to be wary of the advice from a buyer's agent or even a dual agent.

If I counter on price, how low should I go?

What you're really asking here is for the agent's experience. Based on similar situations in the past, should you drop to your rock bottom price? Should you simply come down a very little? Or should you land somewhere in between? Hopefully your agent has had loads of experience and, after sounding out the buyers (or at least the buyers' agent), can tell you how to proceed. Just remember that once you drop your price, it's very hard to raise it back up again.

Do you think I'll be getting more offers soon?

As noted above, buyers' agents will often call the listing agent to say that they're going to be writing up an offer. They do this in the hopes that the listing agent will tell you and you'll hold up on accepting any other offer you may already have in hand. Keep in mind, however, that almost all offers have a time limit. In waiting for another promised offer to come in, the existing offer may expire. [In real life buyers who want the property will often extend their offers for a time if your agent calls them (through their agent) and asks for an extension.]

Will you present my counter?

Listen carefully to how your agent answers. In the past, it would go without saying that the agent would want to meet with the buyers and present your offer to them. In today's market, however, with multiple offers being common, often all your agent plans to do is FAX your counter to the buyers' agent and then to let that person present it. While it's not necessary for your agent to physically present your counteroffer, a lot of negotiating advantage can be lost by not doing so. For example, your agent can see how the buyers react to your counter. Are they really disappointed (meaning they are highly motivated to buy)? Are they relieved that their offer wasn't accepted (meaning they're ready to move on)? Do they immediately begin scrambling to see if they can raise the funds to accept, or come close to accepting your counteroffer? The answer to these questions can help you make your next decision when the buyers counter your counter. However, the only way you'll get it is if your agent presents your counteroffer and is there to see the buyers' reaction.

Have you any suggestions on how to make the deal work?

Sometimes, after countering goes on for a while, it becomes apparent that the two sides are just too far apart. You're asking more than the buyer wants to or can pay. They're offering less than you want or need to accept. It's a stalemate, unless something creative can be thrown into the mix. Don't hesitate to ask your agent to come up with the creative answer. Sometimes it involves a trick in financing. Other times it may be a negotiating maneuver, such as walking away from the table. And sometimes the agent will throw in some of the commission just to make the deal. Don't count on the latter happening every time. But when the agent's commission is 5, 6, or 7 percent, there's a lot of money out there to play with. And many agents will feel it's better to get a smaller piece of the pie than no pie at all.

8

Special Concerns for Condo and Co-Op Sellers

QUESTIONS TO ASK YOURSELF

Am I using an agent?

☐

It's especially hard to sell a condo or co-op by owner. The reason is that often you can't put a sign in front (by the homeowner rules—see below), you may have trouble getting your buyers into the complex, and you may even have trouble finding buyers who understand and want the shared lifestyle. That's why it usually pays to use an agent. This is not to say you *must* use an agent, only that the nature of what you're selling often makes the sale easier with an agent.

Am I promoting my lifestyle?

☐

A condo or co-op is not simply a less (or more) expensive version of a single-family home. It's actually a different kind of lifestyle. And it's important that buyers be informed about this, lest they purchase with unrealistic expectations. Try to be there when buyers come by. By all means show them your unit. But then, take them on a tour of the development and show off the pool/spa, golf range/putting green, recreation building, tennis courts, and so forth. If possible, point out how close your unit is to these facilities. Sometimes buyers may decide to make a purchase not because they fall in love with your unit, but because they like the extra features your development offers. Sometimes they'll buy in spite of your unit to get the amenities!

Do I have a map available showing how to get to the amenities?   ☐

While there are small condo and co-op developments, frequently they are very large covering lots of ground with many buildings. While everything may be familiar to you (since you live there), it could be very confusing to potential buyers, even to agents who bring those buyers by! Therefore, having a good, clear map available especially showing such things as pool/spa, tennis courts, recreation center, parking, your unit, how to get to the street, and so forth can be invaluable. Print some up (you can use your own computer or a store selling such services) and give them to your agent who can hand them out. And leave a stack by your front door so that every buyer who comes by can pick one up. It's an inexpensive yet productive way of helping people get around. After all, you don't want a potential buyer giving up simply because they got lost on the way to the pool!

Have I talked to the HOA, board, and/or architectural committee?   ☐

You're going to need to give your buyer a bunch of information about your development (see below) and most of it will have to come from the board, homeowners' association, and architectural committee. Therefore, it's a good idea to contact them early on. In many cases, they will be ready for you with a packet that contains all the vital information you need. After all, you're probably not the first to come by asking for this information. However, be prepared as they may have a fairly stiff fee ($100 or more) for each packet. Therefore, you'll probably want to give it out only to really serious buyers.

Have I increased the lighting as much as possible?   ☐

A problem with many condos and co-ops is that they are dark inside. This is only natural because most share walls with adjoining units. That means that while there are perhaps windows on the front and rear, there are rarely windows on the sides. As a result, little natural light can trickle in. However, buyers tend to shy away from dark homes.

An old trick when showing homes is to always turn on all the lights. The home appears brighter and more enticing to potential buyers. If your unit is particularly dark, you may want to even go out and purchase extra lamps. You can get very bright, inexpensive floor lamps (around $30 apiece) and set them up in every room. Just make sure that your place is well lit whenever a buyer is likely to come by. (That can mean leaving the lights on when you go out!) It can make all the difference.

Have I turned on the air conditioning/heating?

While it's true for any house that it should be warm in the winter and cool in the summer to attract buyers, it's more important with condos and co-ops where there may be less natural ventilation. Therefore, if you have air conditioning, be sure it's on even when you leave in the summer. And keep the home reasonably warm all the time in the winter. I realize this goes against the grain of many who take pride in conserving energy. However, keep in mind it's only during the sale period, which should be shortened by the fact that you're keeping the home at the right temperature. *Note:* Most salespeople know that buyers are more likely to make an offer if the temperature in the home is slightly cool, perhaps around 68 to 70 degrees Fahrenheit. If you doubt this, think of department or grocery stores that are always cool. Or remember the last time you went out with a salesperson looking at a new car in the summer. Wasn't the first thing the salesperson did was turn on the air conditioning full blast? No, a cool home won't turn a uninterested person into a buyer. But if the person is interested, it might make it easier to get the offer out of him or her.

Have I made my patio area as presentable as possible?

With a single-family home, there's usually side yards and a backyard, not to mention a front yard. With a condo or co-op, there are often no yards! Rather, there may be a small patio area. That's probably the extent of the outside area that goes with the property. Therefore, it's vitally important that this be shown off in the best light. That usually means getting rid of clutter and putting in some good-looking patio equipment. (It doesn't have to be expensive—just clean, with no scratches, marks, or tears.)

It may very well be the case that you never use that patio area. It may even be the case that the future buyers may never use it. But, you can be certain they will at least think about using it when they check out your home. Since it's small, make it shine.

Do I have my neighbor's cooperation?

Neighbors are really important when it comes to a condo or co-op. They're usually a lot closer than in a single-family home. Noises and disturbances can be more easily heard and observed. If you have really bad neighbors who are always throwing loud parties and on whom you've called the HOA or board as well as the police many times, it's something you may need to disclose. However, sometimes you have great neighbors. But, they happen to like to sit outside on their patio, which is right next to yours, and speak loudly. You don't find it objectionable. Your future buyers might not. But, it might be an easier sell if your buyers could see your patio on a quiet day when no one else is right next door talking it up. Therefore, in a nice way, you can ask your neighbors to cooperate when your place is being shown. After all, the person who buys will soon become their next door neighbor and surely they'll want the best people possible moving in.

QUESTIONS TO ASK AN HOA OR BOARD

Do you allow signs on the property?

Since the front yard of a condo is typically owned by everyone in the association, you may not be able to put a sign in front. The reason is that many condominium bylaws preclude you from putting a "For Sale" sign for your condo in any common area and that includes the exterior walls, on doors, or in the windows of your own unit. (Such rules can be hard to enforce, but strict homeowner association boards may try.) Therefore, as soon as you've determined that you want to sell, one of your first trips should be to the homeowners' association or the board of directors to find out about their sign policy. If it's strict, you may want to try and fudge a little. Try putting a sign in the window of your unit. Most people won't complain about that and at least it will help direct a potential buyer to your unit. Sign restrictions are also a good reason to use an agent. The agent can meet buyers at the gate or entrance and then bring them by.

Are there any restrictions on buyers?

In the very distant past some ownership organizations would attempt to restrict buyers on the basis of religion or race. That is outlawed everywhere in the United States today and, in addition, buyers cannot be restricted in terms of health, gender preference, or national origin. Most HOAs are quite progressive and wouldn't dream of doing this. The same holds true for most co-op boards. However, with a co-op there are special considerations when it comes to finances. Many co-ops do restrict buyers in terms of their income levels or their ability to pay their monthly fees. The reason is that the co-op may have a single, large mortgage covering the entire building. If one unit owner fails to pay, then the others must make up the difference. Thus, the other members, through their board, have a vested interest in seeing that your buyer is financially sound. By first talking to the board, or at least the general manager, you will be able to get a sense of what the board is looking for financially in a new buyer, and save yourself a lot of wasted time and effort in bringing in someone who's not fully qualified.

Are there any restrictions on showing the property?

There may be. Usually these restrictions are the same that apply to any guests. The guests may need to park in special areas and avoid creating disturbing noises, and may be limited to certain hours. Since these are usually quite liberal, there probably won't be a problem. Checking with the HOA or board first, however, can't hurt.

Can I allow buyers in the front gate/door?

This can present a problem. If your unit is directly accessible from the street by anyone, then there's no need to be concerned. However, if there is a locked door or gate, then getting potential buyers in becomes more difficult. You probably won't want to hand out the code that opens the door/gate because then almost anyone can come in. And waiting at home all the time so you can open the door/gate for potential buyers can also be tedious and time consuming. Of course, one method may be to list with an agent who will have the access code and who can show the property. However, your problem is not unusual and your HOA or board may have suggestions on how to handle it. If there is a guard or doorkeeper, he or she can be instructed to allow people in to see your unit. Or there may be a special one-time access code that can be used. Be sure to check before simply giving out your own access code to everyone who wants to see your unit.

Can my agent show the property when I'm not there?

One of the big advantages of having an agent is that he or she can show your property for you at any time. Presumably your agent has a key to your front door as well as access to your building or development. Just be sure there's no problem with this from the board or the HOA. Normally there isn't, but sometimes someone on the board or the HOA has been sensitized by a bad incident that happened to them and they will want to restrict access by agents. You may have to argue hard and long to overcome this sort of bias.

Can I put a lockbox on my door?

Usually you can. A lockbox allows not only your own agent, but other subagents, buyers' agents, and anyone in the field who knows the lockbox code to access your home. If your unit is directly accessible from the street, then a lockbox should work fine. If, however, the agents must get through a locked door or gate, the same problems will occur as when buyers themselves want to come by (see above). See how your board/HOA feels about agents other than your own coming by. Most are quite liberal. However, if yours is very strict, you may need to make special arrangements.

How can the buyer get a list of architectural restrictions?

It's important that buyers be provided with a list of architectural restrictions (AR). This is to keep them from coming back later on saying they were duped into buying your unit by thinking they could add on or change it only to find out that they are prevented from doing so. It's a good idea to not only see that they get the architectural restrictions, but you get a signed and dated receipt from them. Of course, you'll need to get a copy of the AR yourself in order to pass it out. Check with your development's architectural committee. Usually a phone call to the chairperson or one of the members will get you a copy. Many states prohibit HOAs and boards from refusing to release this information.

How can the buyer get copies of the CC&Rs, rules, and bylaws?

As with the architectural restrictions, you'll also want to be sure that potential buyers get copies of the conditions, covenants, and restrictions (CC&Rs) that affect the deed. Remember that these are often far more restrictive for a condo or co-op than for a single-family home. Hence, as part of your disclosures you will want to see that the buyers receive the CC&Rs and that you get a receipt. However, you will first have to get them from the board or HOA. (You can usually get the CC&Rs from an escrow company that will obtain them as part of the title search; however, you will probably have to go directly to the association or board for the rules and bylaws.) Most states now provide that these must be given to you. However, you can be charged for the service. Many associations and boards now prepare packets to distribute and typically charge $100 or more for them.

Are there any active lawsuits pending?

Nothing deters buyers (and lenders) more than a lawsuit pending against your association or co-op. In recent years many condos and co-ops have become involved in lawsuits of one sort or another. Sometimes it's the owners suing the builder over defects. Other times it's the board or HOA suing an owner for failure to pay fees. Or an owner suing the development over restrictions. Or owners suing owners over grievances. Depending on who wins and who loses, all of the members of the development might be asked to pay a sometimes sizable judgment. Thus, if you have a lawsuit pending, it could scare away a buyer, or make it difficult for that buyer to obtain necessary financing. Therefore, it's important that you declare to a buyer all lawsuits. This is to protect yourself from that buyer coming back later on trying to get out of the deal and saying you withheld important information about your unit. However, before you can disclose, you must become informed. Most boards and associations will provide this information to you in a general way (parties to the lawsuit are usually in the public domain), but they may not provide the details of the case to protect themselves. It's a good idea to consult with a member of the board or association to learn what's out there and to get some background on it. Thus, when your buyer is alarmed about a lawsuit the board has against the builder, you may be able to explain that it's over leaking roofs and that the insurance will cover most of it, but the board is trying to recover the deductible.

Are there new assessments pending?

This is of particular concern with older developments. It may be time to reroof the complex to the tune of $600,000. However, the reserve fund for roofs only has $100,000 in it. That means that board is going to have to come to the members for the remaining $500,000 as an assessment, which means that monthly fees could skyrocket. It may turn out that this has been a matter of discussion for 6 months; however, you never attended board meetings so you didn't know. At the last meeting it was voted through and will take effect within 2 months. Wouldn't that come as a shock to a buyer who had assumed a low monthly fee only to have it quickly become much higher? And you should have disclosed it because it had already passed the board! Checking with the director of a board or HOA member could keep you out of this pickle.

Are there any known physical problems with the building(s)?

This is going to be a judgment call. It may turn out that people have been complaining for years about the color of the building. Some want it painted white; others want it painted yellow, and so on. It's an ongoing fight at every meeting of the association or board. Yet nothing ever gets done. You may want to inform your buyers about the situation, but it's not something that appears serious. On the other hand, when you check with the board or the association you may learn that all those cracks that have been appearing in the walls, floors, driveways, and walkways are actually a serious problem associated with shifting ground. The board/association has called in experts, but there doesn't seem to be a way to fix it. Some experts have even suggested that the building(s) could fall down in a few years. This is something that you'd want to let buyers know about. But it's also something that you might not have known about until you had contacted the board or association (or scrupulously attended meetings!).

9
Selling "By Owner"

QUESTIONS TO ASK YOURSELF

Do I want to save on the commission?

If you don't, you're the only person on the planet who feels that way! On a $300,000 property, a 6 percent commission is $18,000. That's serious money by almost anyone's standards. Wouldn't you like to pocket that money? And all you have to do is to sell your home on your own. Easy? Hardly. If it were easy nearly everyone would do it. Yet, about 90 percent of homeowners sell through an agent, so there must be good reasons. Of course there are, and they all come down to doing all the work an agent would otherwise do for you. You'll have to go through most of the following steps to sell your home by yourself:

- Fix up the property (which you'll need to do anyway)
- Get a sign
- Advertise
- Show the home
- Negotiate directly with a buyer
- Prepare a sales agreement
- Prepare disclosures
- Handle all other documentation
- Open and manage an escrow

- Possibly help the buyer with financing
- Close the escrow

It's easy to see why it's not easy. Agents do all of the above day in and day out... for them it's routine. (And it's easy to see why they may very well be worth what they charge.) But for someone such as yourself who might do it once every decade, it's mostly unfamiliar and fraught with peril. Nevertheless, if you're a daring soul, you may very well be able to pull it off. It's a decision only you can make.

Do I want to sell faster?

Most people assume it will take longer to sell by owner and very often it does. However, it is possible to shorten the process. The way this is accomplished is by giving all or a portion of the commission you would otherwise save to the buyer. *Consider:* You're selling your home for $400,000. The commission at 6 percent is $24,000. Now let's say instead of paying the commission to an agent, you give it to the buyer. You discount your home $24,000 and offer it at $376,000. Remember, it's a competitive market. Buyers are price sensitive. Who is a buyer more likely to make an offer: to a competitive seller who's listed a similar home for $400,000 with an agent's fee or to you with essentially the same home selling for $376,000? It's something to consider. However, you may be saying, if that were the case, "By Owner" homes would be selling like hotcakes. They probably would. However, most "By Owner" sellers don't offer the discount to the buyer. Rather, they want to keep it all for themselves. And many times they ask above market, because they feel their home is so special. Hence, the fact is, the "By Owner" homes sell much more slowly. It's something else to think about.

Will the market allow me to do it?

You can sell by owner in almost any market. However, you'll sell most easily, and save on the commission, in a hot market where there are lots of buyers competing for fewer homes. On the other hand, if the market's slow, you'll probably get a faster sale by discounting the cost of the commission off the price of the house when selling by owner. The only market in which you won't be able to sell by owner is when it's dead cold (as was the case in the mid-1990s). However, at that time almost no homes were selling in many areas, listed or not.

Do I have the "special skills" necessary to sell?

If you can be pleasant to people, carry on a conversation, and don't get too upset with what people say about something you may be very proud of, then you should be fine. It's incorrect to think that only people who have special skills can sell. I've found that most of the time whatever I'm trying to sell will sell itself. All that I have to do is be pleasant and positive and things move right along. On the other hand, if you're awkward about chatting, would easily be hurt if someone suggested that moose head over your mantle detracted from your home, or just don't feel right about letting strangers look through your things, then perhaps you might be better off listing with an agent. Generally speaking, gregarious people do well selling by owner. Shy people tend not to be so successful.

Am I willing to show my home to strangers?

If you want to save money on the commission (or get a quicker sale by discounting the commission off the price of your home), then you're going to have to show the premises to strangers. (An alternative is to get a fee-for-service broker, if you can find one, to handle the showings for you.) There are really three issues here: security, convenience, and openness.

- There is no real answer to the security issue, although you can attempt to screen potential buyers on the phone, have someone in the house with you when you show it, and remove all valuables before the showing. Nevertheless, in today's world, I don't believe you can eliminate the threat.

- The convenience issue is always going to be there, whether you show the property or you have it listed. Buyers' have little tolerance for your schedule. They want to see the house when they want to see it, else they'll look at some other house. Thus, you'll always need to have the house tidy and ready to show at a moment's notice.

- Openness (also discussed above) is really how you feel about showing your personal things to strangers. Some of us are fine with it. If you're not, then perhaps you ought to list with an agent who can handle the showings for you.

Who will handle the paperwork?

This is often the biggest stumbling block for most people who want to sell by owner. Probably the most important document is the sales agreement. But there are also disclosures to fill out and other documents to deal with. If you've bought and sold a dozen homes, this will seem old hat to you. But, if this is your first or second attempt, then there's still a lot of mystery involved. My suggestion is that you always get a professional to handle the paperwork. When you're dealing with the type of money involved in home sales today, you don't want anything to go wrong. You want it all written down, correctly. Therefore, either hire a good agent to handle the paperwork for you, or hire a good attorney. It's no place for you to be experimenting and practicing on your own.

Do I really have time for this?

It would be a big mistake to think that selling "By Owner" isn't going to take time. Look at the list noted earlier. Each of the things on it will take time, some more than others. If you have a full-time job and/or are raising a family or have other commitments, then I urge you to reconsider. Selling a home on your own is not something that you can devote a few spare hours to when it's convenient for you. You have to do all of the work necessary to find buyers. Then you have to be home to answer their questions when they call. Finally, you must do the work of showing them the property, calling them back, negotiating, and concluding the deal. That doesn't even begin to get into the work involved in closing the transaction. If you are retired and have lots of spare time, or if you work at home, or otherwise can commit time to this task, then by all means move forward. On the other hand, if you're always stressed out because there doesn't seem to be enough hours in the day to complete the tasks at hand, I suggest you may be better off letting an agent handle the sale.

Am I better off hiring a discount broker?

Today discount brokers are sprouting up in many locations. Typically they offer to handle the sale of your property for less than "full service" agents charge. Their fees are often between 4 and 5 percent. While some of these discount brokers, such as Assist2Sell, claim to offer full service at discount by making it up in volume, many will explain that they have cut some of the services they offer. For example, while many discount brokers will list your home on the MLS and do the paperwork, they may expect you to handle the showings and/or pay for advertising. They also may have other work they expect you to do (which, hopefully, is spelled out in their listing contract). *Note:* Even if you list with a discount broker, unless that broker finds the buyer, there will be a buyer's agent involved who will expect to get a commission. If commissions in your area are generally running around 3 percent to the buyer's agent, you want to be careful not to list for less. Thus, if you list for, say, 4 percent, 3 percent would go to the buyer's agent and only 1 percent to the lister. If you list for less than 3 percent to the buyer's agent, then those agents may simply not steer buyers to your property.

What about a fee-for-service broker?

Just a few years ago fee-for-service brokers seemed to be popping out everywhere. Recently, however, they have been harder to find. Here an agent charges you by the service performed. It's just like going in to see a mechanic. There's one price for a brake job, another for a lube and oil, and other prices for an engine overhaul, tune-up, or whatever. The fee-for-service agent also has a list; however, it covers such things as a sign, preparing a sales agreement, handling escrow, negotiating with buyers, showing the property, and so forth. You pay just for what you want... and need. This often jibes very well with "By Owner" sellers who may need just one or two services from an agent. However, the problem that many fee-for-service agents have run into is liability. Their liability in a deal may be just as great if they're receiving $500 for filling out a sales agreement as if they're receiving $15,000 for a full commission. While errors and omissions insurance can help protect them, they nevertheless run the risk of great exposure for a small fee. In addition, sellers who use fee-for-service brokers are likely to blame them if something goes wrong, even if it's the seller's fault. The broker becomes the easiest scapegoat around. Therefore, many of these agents have either dropped out of the business, or have gone back to charging a full or discount commission.

Should I pay for advertising?

You can and you may want to. However, you should be sure that if you do, you have control over what the ad says (in case you're using a fee-for-service broker). When you sell by yourself, you must do everything in your power to let people know your home is for sale. An inexpensive way to accomplish this is to create flyers and put them in a little box on your sign. You can also put up notices on bulletin boards, contact any nearby housing offices of major companies, even go online and leave messages on electronic bulletin boards. I'd be wary, however, of paying money for listing "By Owner" on a For Sale By Owner (FSBO, pronounced *fizz-bo*) site unless I was assured it would have a lot of action. If you're going to advertise in newspapers, be aware that less is usually more. The classic mistake that novice sellers make is saying too much in the ad (consequently paying too much for it as well). As a FSBO seller, you have the magic words "by owner" you can use. Buyers love to check out even very tiny ads that say this in the hope of finding a bargain. Therefore, often all you need do is to create a small three-line ad including:

- "By Owner"
- Number of bedrooms and baths in the house

- Price
- Neighborhood
- Condition of the property
- Your phone number or a number where you can be reached. (You don't necessarily want to put your address in for security reasons.)

Remember, buyers will spend a lot of time going down a long list of tiny ads looking for bargains, so the cost of a big ad might just be wasted.

Can I actually write an ad that sells?

Probably not. However, you don't need to. There are dozens of books out there that tell you how to write a good ad; some that even give you samples of short real estate ads that work. Get down to a library or bookstore, and, for a few bucks, you too can join the wonderful world of advertising!

Where will I get a sign to stick in my front yard?

You could go down to the local drugstore and for $5, pick up a plastic one. However, that would look rather cheap and wouldn't really attract many buyers. Or, you could have a professional looking sign made up at a sign shop for around $75. (Home Depots and other homeware stores sell ready-to-go signs that may include additional offers and services.) If you're selling on your own, you'll want to give your phone number and perhaps a little bit of information on the house, although that's better handled by putting a small box with flyers in it and attaching it to the post. If you're working with a full-service, discount, or fee-for-service broker they should be able to handle the sign for you. *Note:* Be sure your area doesn't have sign restrictions which might limit the size, shape, or location of the sign. Check with a good agent, your homeowners' association, the local planning department, or your board.

Do I really need to bother with flyers?

A good flyer will show a color picture of the house, your phone number, plus most of the important information a buyer wants to know such as number of bedrooms and bathrooms, square footage, and school districts. Of course, it's a bother. You have to snap pictures, get them reproduced, paste (or print) them onto sheets of paper along with all the other information you need. (If you have a computer, a printer, and a digital camera, you're probably home free on doing this yourself.) Just keep in mind that you'll be missing a lot of positive advertising if you skip the flyer.

Should I have a guest book?

Plain and simple, the answer is, Yes! You can ask buyers to sign in and leave their phone number. Most people (when they first come in, not as they're leaving) are more than happy to do this for you. After all, they want to see the house and they assume this is a condition for viewing it. Thus, the next day or so, you can call them back to ask if they liked the home, what they found wrong with it, and if they're interested in making an offer. (Don't overlook this callback; it's one of the biggest deal makers you have.) Another good use of the guest book is that it allows you to exclude buyers to whom you've already talked, if and when you later list the house. You may want to give an exclusive right-to-sell listing (see Chapter 4) to an agent, which means that you'll pay a commission even if you sell the home yourself. However, you exclude those you've already shown it to. Because you found these potential buyers before you listed, should you later sell to them, the agent is not entitled to a commission. You can only do this, however, if you have that guest book where they signed in their name, phone number, and, perhaps, address.

If I get a buyer, do I know how to prepare the sales agreement?

You will need to use a written sales agreement, since in order to be enforceable most real estate contracts must be in writing (Statute of Frauds). However, I suggest you do *not* attempt to fill out the sales agreement yourself. It's complicated and filled with all sorts of legalese that has special meaning in real estate. Get a good agent or an attorney to do it for you. After all, if the buyer's interested in purchasing, it's as much to his or her advantage to be sure the form is correctly filled out.

Do I know how to handle the escrow and closing?

It's not brain surgery. But then again, it's not simple, either.
If you've been through the purchase and sale of a home
several times, you already know the path. A good agent
can help you along the way with any road bumps that may
appear. Just keep in mind that you're probably going to
have to do double-duty. As a "By Owner" seller you're not
only going to have to clear title, which any seller does, but
also you're going to have to follow-up on the buyers to be
sure that they get their necessary financing and that they
remove all their contingencies in a timely fashion. And
you're going to have to keep on top of the escrow officer to
be sure that the title abstract and receipt of documents is
going according to schedule. Can you do it? Probably. But
remember, to accomplish this you'll have to be part com-
forting mother, part taskmaster, and part magician, just
like agents are.

Should I help the buyer with financing?

Today with the best financing in history available, most
real estate purchases are for cash to the seller. The buyer
comes up with a small downpayment, gets a big institu-
tional loan, and cashes you out. But sometimes the buyer
can't qualify or doesn't have any cash. Or maybe you
want to carry financing because you need income (from
the interest on the mortgage) rather than cash to put in
the bank (where it earns very little interest). In that case,
you may indeed help the buyer with the financing. You
may want to or need to give the buyer a second or even a
first mortgage. There are ways to do this while lessening
the risk. However, there is always going to be some risk
when you loan money.

What if the buyer wants my special chair?

This can happen whether you sell by owner or through an
agent. A buyer walks into the home and falls in love with
a piece of your personal property. Maybe it's your favorite
chair. Or it could be the kitchen table, or a bedroom set, or
whatever. Obviously, the article is not intended to go with
the house. But the buyer wants it so badly that he or she
insists on having it. The buyer writes into the purchase

agreement a contingency saying that the sale is subject to your special chair being included. What should you do? The smart thing to do is to realize that the old beaten up chair you're sitting in (and that your spouse has been threatening to haul to the dump) just became a deal point. Okay, you tell the buyer he or she can have the chair, but it's going to cost. You raise the price or change the terms or timing or whatever. The chair is like money that just dropped into your lap. That's the smart way. Of course, there's the emotional way. Your chair is like Linus's blanket (of Peanuts fame). You can't live without it. You have to have it. Now you've made the chair a deal point and in order to get it you may have to make concessions to the buyer, such as lowering your price. If possible, it's important to remember that what we're dealing with here are things… inanimate objects that don't have any feelings. If possible, try to separate yourself from their emotional hold on you; else, pay the price.

Should I offer to co-broke?

As soon as you put a "By Owner" sign in the front yard, you're sure to start getting calls from agents who want to list your property. They'll call asking if there's any way they can help you sell your house. Of course, what they're really hoping is that if they help you out, you'll eventually list with them. Eventually some may call who say they're working with a buyer who might very well be interested in the house. Will you "co-broke"? This simply is asking whether you'll pay them a buyer's agent's commission (half the regular commission) if they come by with a buyer who eventually purchases your home. If you would otherwise pay 6 percent, for example, they will want 3 percent. You have to ask yourself if it's worth 3 percent to sell your home. (Besides, they may be willing (though not always) to handle much of the paperwork for you.) Unless the market is very hot, I'd be sorely tempted not to accept their offer and co-broke my property. A quick sale may be worth paying the half-commission. Just be sure, however, that the listing agreement they will want you to sign is for a short period of time, just enough so they can bring their buyer by (perhaps a day or two). You probably won't want to sign a 3- or 6-month listing in this situation.

Have I set a time limit?

If you decide to sell by owner, this is probably the most important thing you can do. Think of the whole process as a learning experience or at least as an experiment. You're going to give something new a try. However, like all learning experiences and experiments, it should have a definite ending time. Say to yourself that you'll try selling your home on your own for 3 weeks, or 3 months, or however long you decide. But write that number down when you start. And keep looking at it. And if the time expires and you still haven't sold your home, tell yourself that you gave it the "old college try," that you did your best (even if you didn't!), and move on with your life. Find a good agent and list. The worst thing you can do is to get bogged down for months (or years!) trying to sell that old house. Bite the bullet, list, hopefully sell, and move on. It may end up costing a bit more than you had hoped, but money isn't everything.

10

Selling Under Pressure (If The Market Should Drop)

QUESTIONS TO ASK YOURSELF

Have I analyzed where the market is?

We don't sell our homes in a vacuum. We have to cater to the competition, to the marketplace. And often whether we make a profit or sustain a loss has less to do with how nice our property is and more to do with where the market is. During the early years of this century, the real estate market was the hottest in recent history. Some areas of the country were recording an astounding 25 percent price appreciation, year after year. On the other hand, for most of the 1990s, real estate was in the doldrums. In many areas property prices declined, sometimes as much as 30 percent. How well you did depended a lot on *when you sold.* The easiest way to check out the current market is to do three things: (1) Ask an agent. Most agents are quite forthright and will tell you how things are. (However, you may notice that before they get you to list they might make the market sound a bit rosier than when you're ready to list and are trying to decide on a price, when they might make the market sound a bit gloomier.) (2) Read the local newspaper. Reporters love to write stories on real estate, particularly if the market's strongly up or down. Look for these stories in the business section. (3) Compare housing inventory. Any good agent can get these statistics for you (see Chapter 3). They show how many houses are currently for sale in your area and how long the estimated time is to sell out the inventory. Compare year-to-year stats. Generally speaking, 3 to 6 months to sell the inventory is considered about normal. Six to eighteen months is bad. And anything like 2 months or less is considered extraordinarily hot.

Is it likely to get better or worse?

Now it's time to take your best guess. No one knows where the market will go. However, this can be an important question to ask since, if the market's getting better, you may want to hold off selling for a while until prices rise. And, if it's getting worse, you may want to sell immediately before prices fall further. You can get opinions from agents, from reporters in newspaper articles, from economists at colleges, and of course, comments from the government which can often be tainted to favor whatever party happens to be in power. However, at the end of the day, the fact remains that no one really knows. So take your best guess.

How much do I owe upon the sale of the property?

While the price you can get for your property is determined by ups or downs in the marketplace, before putting your home on the market it's worthwhile to get a pretty solid figure. Your lender(s) provide information on your mortgage payoffs. Just remember, these payoff amounts change as you make each monthly payment. Your agent should be able to provide you with an estimate of transaction costs. These may include property taxes you owe, your commission, escrow and title costs, and so on. Add all of these figures together and that's how much comes off the top of any sale before you can put a dime into your own pocket.

What if I sell "by owner"?

The biggest cost of selling that's a variable is the real estate commission. You can't change the amount you owe (for an exception, see "short sale" below). The escrow and title fees are pretty much set. And all the remaining costs are usually minor. Therefore, the one area where you can cut your costs dramatically is to sell the home on your own. Unfortunately, while that's easier in a hot market, it's far harder in a cold market. Nevertheless, it's an alternative to consider. (Reread Chapter 9.)

How much can I realistically get when I sell?

Now it's time to remove the blinders and start making some very close calculations. Reread Chapter 3 on pricing and try to get a good idea of where your house should be priced. Keep in mind, however, that when the market's down, or falling, the price your neighbor received for a similar house may not be the amount you realize. In the interval between the time your neighbor sells and when you sell, prices could have dropped. Hence, you might figure on getting a few percent less (or however much seems reasonable). Of course, in a rising market, it works just the other way around.

Do I have equity or am I "upside down"?

Once you know how much you will owe on the sale and how much you can expect to get, you can make that critical calculation. If what you owe is less than what you are likely to get, you'll walk away with some cash in your pocket. How much, of course, depends on how big the difference between what you owe and what you can get. On the other hand, if you owe more than your house is worth, you're in trouble. In the industry, this is called being "upside down." In order to sell, you will either have to pay cash out of your pocket, or make some other kind of creative arrangement. All of the following questions in this section assume that you are upside down and suggest ways of coping with the situation.

Have I talked to my lender?

Keeping the lines of communication open is vital if you are to protect yourself in real estate. You may be caught up on your payments, or you may be behind. But, if you're behind, you want to be sure that your lender knows that you're not trying to skip out and that you're working hard to catch up. If you're upside down, you want to make your lender aware of this fact. Just because the market and falling prices may make it perfectly obvious to you that your home isn't worth as much as you owe on it, don't assume the lender knows. As long as a loan is performing (you're making the payments), lenders count it as an asset and almost never check up on the property. Your equity could be plus $100,000 or minus $100,000 and a lender would never know, as long as you keep making the payments. However, if you're upside down, you'd be wise to explain this to your lender, especially if you're not able to keep up with your payments. Your lender may prove surprisingly flexible by offering to rewrite the loan, thus advancing you more money; temporarily reducing your payments; eliminating your payments for a number of months until you can catch up; and much more. Don't always, however, attribute this generosity to the goodwill of the lender. In many cases the federal government, which may be underwriting your loan, may demand that lenders seek ways in which to mitigate problem borrowers. Your lender may have a solution for you... but you won't know until you ask.

Have I talked to an agent?

One of the things that we might mistakenly do is assume that we know the answer even before we ask the question. Hence, we don't even ask. Don't fall into this trap. Even though you're confident you know how much you owe and have worked out pretty clearly (at least in your mind) what your home is worth, be sure to check with a good agent. You could be very surprised by what you find out. The agent may recheck your figures and discover that your equity is larger, or smaller. Or, the agent may know of someone looking for a home just like yours who is willing to give you a quick sale. Or perhaps the agent may suggest some creative financing that might help you get out of your dilemma. Of course, you'll never know unless you ask.

Have I talked to my financial advisor?

While your home may represent your largest, single financial asset, it is undoubtedly not your only asset. If you find you want/need to sell and the market is against you, you should speak with your financial advisor about alternative solutions. For example, your advisor may suggest selling other assets in order to keep your house until the market turns for the better. Selling such items as an extra car, a boat, motorcycle, or other personal asset may give you enough money to keep going longer. Another alternative suggested may be to refinance the property. Be wary of using cash advances on your credit card to support your home. These are intended to be short-term loans and typically carry high interest rates which can put you even deeper in debt. Also, be wary of cashing in bonds, stocks, and other savings which may be part of your long-term financial plan, including retirement.

Have I talked to my attorney?

An attorney can be helpful if you're being badgered by a lender. A letter on a lawyer's stationery can sometimes make lenders much more cordial. The attorney also may have creative solutions to the problem of selling a home in a down market, particularly if you're upside down. And the attorney can offer you legal alternatives including a description of the foreclosure process. So be sure to ask. Of course, attorneys are often expensive, but you can probably arrange a set fee for a set amount of time and advice. And that could be money well spent.

Am I current on my payments?

Being current can be both good and bad. The best way to protect your credit is to always make payments on time, and especially to a mortgage lender. However, if you're in a dire situation, upside down and unable to sell, and need your lender's cooperation in securing a "deed in lieu of foreclosure" or a "short sale" (described below), being behind in payments can be a useful tool. Most lenders will not even listen to your pleas for relief as long as you're all paid up. After all, why should they? Your payment record indicates you'll continue making payments no matter what. All they have to do is sit tight and collect the interest every month. On the other hand, if you're behind, particularly if you're more than a month or two behind, the lender is going to be more attentive. Being behind indicates that you may not be able to continue making payments. The lender might need to foreclose. And the last thing most lenders want is a "nonperforming" mortgage.

Being behind in payments is a way of getting your lender's attention. However, keep in mind it will also surely have a deleterious effect on your credit.

Is the bank threatening foreclosure?

Being upside down is one thing. Being threatened with foreclosure is another. You get the former when you owe more than your house is worth, usually because of a turn in the market or because of overfinancing. You get the latter usually when you don't make your payments as agreed. A combination of both can be financially deadly. You should know when your lender threatens foreclosure. Typically it's after you're behind payments a few months. Most lenders will send out letters and make calls notifying you of your delinquency and demanding back payment plus penalties of what you owe. How long lenders will keep this up varies, but eventually they will send you a notice of default, which indicates you are in violation of your mortgage contract. This is typically the first step to foreclosure. In a "deed of trust" state, foreclosure may take as little time as a few months. In a state where a true mortgage is used, it can take far longer. You should know what type of instrument you have. If not, a title insurance company should be able to research it for you. Or a call to your lender should give you the information. Check with a good agent or attorney for the actual procedure used in your state. Keep in mind that to avoid foreclosure, you must be very careful of deadlines. Failure to respond or meet a deadline could mean the loss of your home.

Have I considered a "deed in lieu of foreclosure"?

Prior to the 1990s, this was seldom used. However, so many borrowers became upside down that it came into common use. Simply put, instead of going through the lengthy and costly foreclosure process, a lender allows you to deed the property to it. You get out from under, so to speak; the lender gets your home and you can start over. A deed in lieu, however, is not without its problems. The two biggest concerns are (1) trouble convincing a lender to give it to you. Many times lenders will refuse to allow a deed in lieu and will instead pursue a formal foreclosure. One reason they may want to do this is if you have other assets. Normally, a house is the collateral for a mortgage. But, if at foreclosure, sale of the house doesn't bring enough money to pay back the lender in full, it may be possible for the lender to secure a deficiency judgment. This can be used to attach your other assets. [*Note:* Deficiency judgments are normally only possible if the lender does a judicial (goes to court) foreclosure.] (2) A deed in lieu sends a bad credit signal when you later want to obtain other financing. Decades ago when deeds in lieu were a novelty, they were rarely reported to credit bureaus. But in hard times, lenders typically report them. While usually not as bad as having a foreclosure reported against your credit, it can be almost as bad. Thus, getting a deed in lieu can harm your credit for years to come.

Have I considered asking for a short sale?

A "short sale" is where the lender agrees to take less than is owed. For example, (forgetting transaction costs for the moment), your home is worth $250,000. But you owe $275,000. In a short sale, the lender accepts $250,000 as payment in full so that the home can be sold. If you're upside down you may want to suggest to the lender that the best way for both of you to get out of this predicament is for you to remain in the property, keeping it in good shape, finding a buyer, and then selling for less than market with the lender accepting less than owed. The problem, of course, is that the lender is going to be less than thrilled. A short sale means a loss on the books for the mortgage company. Therefore, most lenders, at least initially, will refuse a short sale. However, if you do find a buyer ready, willing, and able to purchase on a short sale, write up the deal (or have your agent write it), get a deposit, and present it to the lender. Now it's a different story. From the lender's perspective, in a market where real estate prices are falling and you've made it clear you can't hang onto the house, it's really tough to turn such a deal down, provided the amount short is not too great. After all, you're offering a way out that's neat and clean. If the lender refuses, there's the dirty way, involving foreclosure and the costs of fixing up a property that the lender could get in damaged condition. (*Note:* See above on making your payments on time. One risky way to help convince a lender that you won't simply keep on making payments is to be behind in them.)

Have I considered renting out the property?

Instead of selling at a loss or losing the home to foreclosure, you may want to consider turning it into a rental. If the rental market is good in your area, you may be able to rent out the property to handle most or all of the mortgage—principle, interest, taxes, and insurance (PITI). You then move someplace else (you're going to have to move anyhow, aren't you) and keep your house afloat from rental income. If you choose to do this, read up on how to rent real estate. You'll want to scrupulously select your tenants, to be sure they can afford the rent and won't make a mess. And you'll need to set aside money for repairs and maintenance as they come up. Being a landlord is no easy task, but it can be a much better alternative than foreclosure.

Have I considered staying where I am?

Some sellers, realizing that they can't sell or easily get out from under, have made significant changes in order to avoid losing their home. They have refused job transfers, have taken lower-paying jobs, have borrowed money (from the bank or relatives)—all so that they could stay were they were. In some desperate cases, this has meant using up some of the retirement money or the kids' college funds. And the result can mean a lesser lifestyle, for awhile—all to avoid foreclosure and losing a home in a bad market. However, in the past, things have almost always turned around, and usually within a few years. Even the Great Depression of the 1930s led to the hyper real estate market of the late 1940s and 1950s. The great real estate recession of the 1990s turned into the amazing real estate boom of the twenty-first century. Hanging on can lead to better things. On the other hand, you might not be able to hang on long enough. Or you might be able to simply dump the house and move onto a better life elsewhere. It's a difficult call to make.

Have I considered "trading places"?

Here's a novel idea. You're in trouble with your home. You have to leave the area to keep your job. Yet you can't sell because your home is upside down. And you can't rent because the market is too bad. Chances are you're not alone. There might very well be someone in a similar pickle where you're moving to. A small ad might attract them and you could simply trade homes for awhile. A perfect solution? Hardly. You never know, they might trash your house. On the other hand, if you're going to lose it anyway…

Am I thinking about "walking"?

Many people see this as their last alternative. If they can't make their payments, they'll just get all their things, close the door behind them, and move on. You can do this, too. However, if you hope to buy another house in the future, you'd be wise to reconsider. Walking almost certainly directs a huge red flag at your credit. You'll find that getting any credit in the future, particularly a mortgage, will become very difficult. Sometimes it's best not to even think of this as an option.

QUESTIONS TO ASK A LENDER

Will you help me refinance?

In recent years we've had a revolution in the lending industry. People who before could never qualify for a mortgage now routinely can get one, albeit sometimes at a higher interest rate. It may be the case that a solution to your financial/housing problem is to refinance. With the cash infusion you could get by cashing out your equity, you might have enough money to fix up your property so it's easier to sell, to keep going until you get a better job, or otherwise straighten yourself out. Of course, if you already have a high mortgage on your property, you may feel that you don't have enough equity to handle a refinance. Don't assume this until several lenders have told you so. Today there are mortgages readily available for 90, 95, 100, and even 103 percent of the value of your home! Indeed, in some cases mortgages of 125 percent of the value have been made, but usually in strong rather than weak markets. Check with a lender, and not just the one who currently holds your mortgage. You just might get a pleasant surprise.

Will you give me a second mortgage?   ☐

Even if your (or another) lender won't refinance your existing loan, they might be willing to give you a second mortgage. Seconds typically are riskier than firsts (which is
what your big mortgage probably is) and, as a result, usually carry a higher interest rate, which is why lenders like
them. Sometimes a lender who won't refinance, will offer
you a second. *Note:* It's important to understand the order
of mortgages. The "first" is the first mortgage placed on the
property. The "second" is the second placed on the property… and so on. This order is important because in foreclosure and a forced sale, all of the money from the sale
first goes to pay the first mortgage. Only if there is something left over does anything go to pay the second, then
third, and subsequent mortgages. That's why seconds are
considered riskier and require a higher interest rate.

Will you defer payments for awhile?   ☐

As noted earlier, lenders are encouraged to do this by the
government, providing you can demonstrate that after a
period of time you'll be able to continue making payments. (The lost interest is sometimes added onto the top
of the loan or—rarely—forgiven.) For example, you may
have been sick and fallen behind. But now you're well.
Only you owe so much that even though you're back at
work, you can't make up the payments. A lull in payments of 3 or 4 months is all you'd need to get you back
on your feet. A lender just might see things your way.

Will you accept a deed in lieu?   ☐

You won't know until you ask. However, keep in mind that
the only reason a lender would do this is if it's to the
lender's advantage. You have to give the lender reasons
why giving you a deed in lieu makes more sense than letting you stay in the property during the foreclosure process.

Will you accept a short sale?   ☐

You can ask, but expect a quick "No." The reason is that
no lender wants to take a loss. This is particularly the case

when you're suggesting a hypothetical loss. In other words, you're asking if you can find a buyer at a price lower than the mortgage value. After all, if the lender says, "Yes," who knows how much lower you'd want to go? On the other hand, if you've got a buyer ready, willing, and able to purchase, the lender might see things very differently. Asking with a purchase contract in hand for a short sale might just get a positive response.

Are you going to proceed with foreclosure?

Usually the first step is a notice of default, often hand-delivered (or sent by mail requiring your signature). However, if you've kept the lines of communication open with your lender, you may be informed that this is coming well in advance. And this knowledge can help you plan a strategy to avoid it.

What is the foreclosure process?

Your lender knows very well and should share all the details with you. (If you can't get this information from your lender, ask a good real estate agent or attorney in your state.) However, be wary of scare tactics. A few lenders will go out of their way to make phone calls emphasizing the dire consequences of foreclosure to your credit, your economic, and even your physical health. Be aware that lenders want the easy solution for them —for you to just keep on making payments.

11
Closing the Sale

QUESTIONS TO ASK YOURSELF

Do I understand what an escrow is?

☐

If you are new to real estate, opening an escrow can seem strange and foreign. (If you're an old hand, skip this question and move on!) When you buy a jar of mayonnaise, a stock, or even a car, the transaction is closed in a few minutes. In real estate, on the other hand, as soon as you and the buyers agree on the deal, an escrow is opened and it can take weeks, sometimes months, to close that escrow and conclude the sale. Why? The reason is that selling real estate involves processes that take time. It takes time for you (through a title company) to search the title and to clear any clouds (problems) that may affect it. It takes time for the buyers to get financing and conduct inspections. It takes time to fix any physical problems with the property. And so on. Without an escrow, most deals would fall apart because buyers and sellers would have to work directly with each other over these matters as well as directly handling the money. Issues of trust, responsibility, and even convenience would poison the water. With an escrow, these matters don't arise (usually) because the escrow is the equivalent of a neutral stake holder who handles all the monies and documents during the time all these things are being accomplished.

144

Do I know the date of closing?

Time is the essence of a real estate closing. The sales agreement should specify the amount of time given to conclude the purchase, that is, the date at which the escrow is scheduled to close. The typical time is 30 days, although any amount of time can be chosen. That's the time during which the buyers need to get financing and remove contingencies, and you need to clear title and do any required clean-up work. The question always arises of what happens if that date is not met. Technically, if escrow fails to close by the closing date, then the deal is off. Depending on what happened during the escrow period and how your contract was written, the buyers may or may not be entitled to the return of their deposit. For example, if the contract contained a typical financing contingency and the buyers couldn't get a loan, they would normally be entitled to receive their entire deposit. On the other hand, if all contingencies were removed and they simply failed to close, then you may be entitled to keep the deposit (which is usually split with your agent). In real life, there's usually a little bit of give over the date. If escrow closes within a few days of the target date, all is often forgiven and the deal moves forward. However, some sellers who want to get out of the contract (perhaps they've received a better back-up offer), may want to use failure to meet the exact date for closing as a reason for scuttling the deal. If you're in that position, then it's time to check with your attorney about your options.

Has escrow been opened?

Escrow doesn't happen by itself. Someone must go to an escrow company, present the sales agreement, and open escrow. Typically this is your agent or the buyer's agent. It only takes a few minutes to open escrow; however, if you're the one paying for it, you should take the time to determine the cost. It may save you a considerable amount of money if you shop around a bit before committing to one particular escrow company.

Have I signed the preliminary escrow instructions?

Shortly after escrow is opened, the escrow officer will draw up a set of instructions to the escrow and you will be asked to sign them. These instructions are based on the sales agreement and specify what monies, documents, and other items escrow is ordered to process before concluding the deal. In some sense these instructions simply repeat the sales agreement. However, since they are drawn up by a person, they are open to interpretation. Therefore, you should read them very carefully to be sure they correctly represent the intent of the sales agreement. Sometimes an escrow officer can misunderstand what you and the buyer agreed on. For example, you're giving the buyer an *up to* $5000 roof allowance, depending on the results of a roof inspection, and it comes out as a $5000 credit regardless of the roof inspection. If that misunderstanding is reflected in the preliminary escrow instructions, it can be hard to correct later on. Also, these preliminary instructions often contain a clause that says there will be a fee paid to escrow *even if the deal never closes*. Once you sign, you're committed to pay. You may want to negotiate this clause out, or at least commit to paying a reduced fee if the deal falls through.

Is my agent taking charge of the closing?

One of the important things you're paying a commission to an agent for is to manage the closing. Your agent should do all of the following (unless you've negotiated a reduced commission for reduced service, or a fee-for-service situation in which it may become your responsibility):

- Open escrow (or see that it's opened)
- Follow the buyer's progress in securing financing
- Follow the buyer's progress in removing contingencies in a timely fashion
- Check the Abstract of Title for problems (see below)
- Provide you with disclosures and deliver them to escrow

- Arrange for a termite inspection and others as may be needed
- Provide any additional items escrow needs
- Keep you informed of any problems or concerns

If you sense that your agent is not performing the job as expected, you should feel free to contact the escrow officer yourself. You'll quickly learn if everything is on track, or if things have been allowed to slide by. In a worst case scenario, in order to save the deal, you may have to step in and do what you expected your agent to do.

Are there any loose ends left up to me?

When escrow opens and at least once a week thereafter, be sure and ask both the escrow officer and your agent if there's something that you're expected to do. In theory they should come to you with problems as they occur. However, sometimes people get busy and simply put your escrow on the back burner. (This is not to excuse their action—it's simply a fact of the real estate business.) When you discover that there is something for you to do, for example, repair water damage in a bathroom discovered as a result of the termite/pest inspection, get right on it. Remember, time is critical. You may only have a few weeks left to close the deal, and it may take every bit of that time to get a permit, a contractor to do the work, and a reinspection. If you wait until the last moment, escrow may not be able to close because work you were to do didn't get done. Now the onus is on you.

Has the buyer increased the deposit?

The very nature of real estate transactions today suggests that until the contingencies are removed, there really is no deal. For that reason a deposit does not carry the "earnest money" weight it used to. In the past, as soon as a buyer put up a deposit, it was at great risk. Today, however, with the sale subject to the buyer's approving disclosures and inspections and getting financing, there's really not much of a deal at first. Hence, since the deposit isn't at such great risk, its size isn't as important. However, as the contingencies are removed and the deal solidifies, the deposit is at increasingly greater risk for the buyer. Perhaps 3 weeks or so into the deal, with most of the contingencies removed, if the buyer was to try and back out, he or she would stand a good chance of losing it. It's at this point that the size of the deposit can become an important factor. Hence, some contracts will call for the buyer to increase the size of the deposit after contingencies are removed. In a simple deal that will close shortly after contingencies are removed, this is probably not so important. But in a transaction with a long escrow, perhaps waiting for complicated financing, increasing the deposit helps lock the buyer into the deal. If your sales agreement calls for the buyer to increase the deposit at a certain point, be sure he or she does. It will help to ensure that your sale will eventually close, or that you could have a sizeable deposit to split with your agent!

Are there any problems with the buyer's loan?

You might reasonably say to yourself that this is the buyer's problem, so why should it concern me? The answer, of course, is that if the buyer doesn't get a mortgage, he or she probably won't be able to close the deal and your sale will fall through. Since there is undoubtedly a financing contingency written into the purchase agreement, if the buyer is unable to secure funding monies, not only could the buyer back out of the transaction, but he or she could get the full deposit back as well! Not a happy situation for the seller who has probably taken the house off the market for a month or more and has incurred other expenses fully expecting the deal to close. Therefore, it's to *your* advantage to keep an eye on the buyer's loan. You should check with either the buyer's agent, or the buyer directly (either through your own agent or by yourself), at least once a week to see how things are coming. Any hint of a problem such as, "There are a few bumps in the road," or "We're almost past the qualifying problem," should alert you to trouble. The buyer can be approved for financing within a day or so (and should have been before the sale); hence, the suggestion of any small problem here may be the tip of the iceberg. You may offer to help by carrying some of the financing yourself, if you're able and inclined to do so. On the other hand, you may want to prepare your house to go back on the market if a serious problem develops. Of course, you won't know unless you pay attention to the buyer's loan status.

Have I prepared and given all needed disclosures to the buyer?

As noted in Chapter 5, you will undoubtedly need to give the buyer disclosure statements. These will include a disclosure with regard to lead and other any environmental hazards as mandated by the federal and your state governments. You'll also probably be required (either by your state or the purchase contract) to provide disclosures about the property. Have you prepared all of these and delivered them to the buyer? Has the buyer acknowledged receipt of them by signing and dating each disclosure? Remember, many disclosures are time-sensitive. The buyer has days, sometimes weeks, to back out of the deal without penalty from the time of receipt of the disclosures. The last thing you should want is to have those disclosure statements sitting in a desk drawer gathering dust. Delays caused by failing to promptly deliver them to the buyer could cost you the deal.

Is the buyer working on removing contingencies?

Checking with your agent, who will check with the buyer's agent, should let you know. Also, you'll know if the buyer fails to meet any deadlines. For example, the buyer may have 2 weeks to give you active notice that he or she has inspected the property and approved the report, hence removing the professional inspection contingency. If the 2 weeks pass and there's no approval, you may no longer have a deal. Of course, it could just be an oversight and the buyer may be panicking trying to get the papers to you. On the other hand, maybe you've gotten a better back-up offer and would love a graceful way to back out of the deal, and hence will want to stick with the strict deadline! Keep track of how well the buyer is removing the contingencies both to keep your deal on track and to sometimes provide you with a way out.

Are there any problems with the house?

Usually you'll be the first to know. The buyer doesn't like the fact that you've disclosed cracks in the foundation. Or he or she won't approve an inspection report because it says the house has faulty wiring. Often, but not always, this is dumped right back in your lap. Now, to save the deal, you must do something. That something could be a corrective fix, or it might involve crediting the buyer with some more money, or…. The point here is that it's important to know if there are problems with the house and then work with your agent, the buyer's agent, and perhaps even your attorney, to work them out.

Are there any "clouds" on my title?

Nope, it's not a weather condition. "Clouds" refer to anything that prevents you from giving "clear" title to the buyer. It could be something as complex as a right-of-way dispute over a portion of your land. Or it could be as unexpected as a judgment against you from a bank or other creditor. Often when we pay back loans we expect the creditor to remove the loan from our records. But sometimes creditors make mistakes and the loan remains and eventually filters down through the company until an attorney takes it to court and secures a judgment against you. That judgment may be filed against your home, and it can sit there for years until you decide to sell and it suddenly appears. Now, you can either pay it off from the proceeds of the sale, or, if it's been placed in error, you can go back to the original creditor to have it removed. (Sometimes going back a decade or more to a creditor which by now may be out of business can be a real hassle!) The point here is that until you can give clear title to the property, usually you won't be able to close the sale. Hence, as soon as a cloud appears, take care of it one way or another. (Sometimes it is possible to leave enough money in escrow, which then remains open, to handle a judgment against you, thus allowing the sale to proceed.)

Have I called in a pest control company?

Remember, in most cases the seller must provide a termite clearance and the only way to get that is by having an inspection. Thus, it's up to you (or your agent) to call the pest control people. Usually they will come within a week or less. Keep in mind, however, that in most parts of the country termites are ubiquitous. That means you are likely to have them and they are likely to have caused damage. Thus you'll probably need to proceed with some repair work and some extermination, both of which take time. Even after you call in a pest control company, pay special attention to their report and move quickly in getting necessary work done. *Note:* If you are not sure the buyer is going to be able to go through with the purchase, you may want to hold up a bit on expensive work. On the other hand, if you're planning to sell the house soon to another buyer, if not this one, why not just bite the bullet and get it done? Also see Chapter 6.

Do I need to consult with an attorney?

There are two rules when it comes to attorneys. The first is, if you have to ask yourself if you need one, you probably do. And if you do, you probably needed one a long time ago. If you originally had an attorney prepare, or at least check, your sales agreement, you should be on pretty good ground now. You may want the attorney to check both your preliminary and final escrow instructions as well as any documents you are asked to sign. And an attorney may be very helpful in removing clouds on the title. On the other hand, it usually doesn't take an attorney to get a termite clearance or to fix a roof. Use common sense, but err on the side of being safe.

Does my agent call me regularly and keep me informed?

You have to ask yourself this question. If the answer is positive, then chances are you have a good agent and your closing is progressing smoothly… or you're aware of any problems that are cropping up. On the other hand, if your agent seldom calls, you should consider it a warning signal. When closing a deal, don't assume that no news is good news. Actually, it's often the other way around. No news may mean someone is afraid of telling you bad news. If your agent doesn't call you at least once a week to update you, call your agent. And then your escrow officer to confirm what your agent says. If you're not satisfied with what you hear, step in to the closing yourself to expedite whatever the problem(s) happens to be. Don't be shy here. Taking charge while there's still time left to do something may just be what it takes to save your deal.

Is my home ready for the final "walk-through"?

As part of the closing process, the buyers (in the purchase agreement) may have insisted upon a final walk-
through. This gives them the opportunity to check out
the property just before the escrow closes to see that it's
in at least as good a shape as it was when they made their
offer (and you accepted). In truth, however, the final
walk-through can be an opportunity for you to avoid
problems after the sale, provided you handle it correctly.
Ideally, you should make the home spic-and-span. And if
any problems have developed, such as a broken appliance, you should point it out and offer to repair it. The
whole purpose of the final walk-through is to get things
out in the open *before* the escrow closes and it's too late
for you to easily do something about them. (If you wait
until after the closing it often becomes a matter of "did it
happen before or after closing?," and expensive fixes can
be demanded by buyers with attorneys sometimes getting involved.) A word of caution, however. Sometimes
buyers will attempt to use the final walk-through as a
way of either getting out of the deal, or reopening the
negotiations so they can get a better price. Typically, this
occurs when they begin finding fault with all sorts of
things that either are not broken or damaged, or were so
before the sale and were pointed out to them. Your agent
can perform a very useful service here by pointing out to
the buyers that their behavior is inappropriate, that the
final walk-through is intended only to see if something
new is actually wrong. (Having pictures or, sometimes
better, having a few other people who can speak to your
claims of the original condition of the property can seriously bolster your case.) If the buyers won't budge and
refuse to close, and you feel their position is not war-
ranted by the condition of the property, it's probably
time to call in the lawyers.

Do I have to pay escrow and title fees?

Asking after escrow has opened is like a skydiver won-
dering if she has a parachute after she's jumped. Remember, who pays for escrow charges and title insurance is
decided either by custom in your area, or if it was a deal

point, by what the purchase agreement specified. If the purchase agreement called for you to pay these charges, then you will almost certainly have to. On the other hand, if the agreement specified that you were not to pay these charges (or did not address them directly, which would be very unusual), then you might not have to. Remember to check the preliminary escrow instructions in which you may have agreed to pay the charges.

Do I know the dollar amount of the commission?

It should be an easy thing to calculate. The commission is, for example, 5 percent of a $150,000 sales price or $7500. Right? But, what if you're giving the buyers a $10,000 credit which means that you're actually receiving only $140,000? Or what if the buyers are purchasing all your furniture for $15,000, meaning that you're getting $165,000? What now is the dollar amount of the commission? The way most listings are written (you should always refer back to the listing agreement you signed), the dollar amount of the commission is for the purchase price specified on the purchase agreement. But, not always. Be sure to double check. And then, be sure the dollar amount to be paid is correct on both the preliminary and final escrow statements.

Do I understand "prorations"?

A part of your closing costs usually involve prorations. It's important that you understand that prorations, properly handled, are not an expense nor a fee. Prorations are based on a certain date, typically, though not necessarily, the close of escrow. As of that date a kind of inventory is taken. If you've paid taxes, insurance, or other items that the buyers may be taking over, beyond that date, the buyers owe you a refund. Your payments are "prorated" as of the close of escrow, and you get a credit on your escrow statement. On the other hand, if you owe payment on taxes, insurance, or other items and these are paid out of escrow by the buyers, then you owe them a refund. Don't worry about the calculations themselves, although you will certainly want to check the math and the dates. Escrow officers deal with prorations day in and day out and are usually quite capable when it comes to handling them.

Have I been told the "home warranty plan" charge?

Very often the seller will be asked (by your agent, the buyer's agent, or the buyer) to provide a home warranty insurance plan. This plan pays for most repairs to appliances and other home systems (such as plumbing and electric) that occur after the sale. (Sometimes you can buy a policy that applies to the home prior to the sale.) These policies usually have a deductible, typically around $50 for covered items. And the seller usually pays. Why, you may be asking, should I pay for an insurance plan for the buyer? The reason is that it keeps you from having to pay directly for items that break shortly after the sale. The most common example is the water heater. Surprisingly, often a water heater will go out (leak) within months of the sale. The buyer will claim that it was defective, that the seller should have known about it, and that he or she should pay for its repair. Since installing a new water heater can easily cost $500 or more, it's not a cheap item. Of course, as a seller you could always claim that it was working perfectly when you left the home. This usually leads to acrimonious behavior between buyer and seller. To smooth things over, in the past, real estate agents would many times reach into their pockets to cover the cost. Hence, today it's not hard to understand why these same agents are encouraging sellers to pay for the cost (typically around $350, depending on what you insure) of the warranty insurance, which will cover most of the cost of a new heater. Should you get it? To my way of thinking, it's a cheap way of avoiding complications after the sale.

Do I know of any extra charges?

Unfortunately, in today's world of closing real estate transactions, extra charges (sometimes called "garbage fees") are rampant. These can add up to a sizeable chunk of cash. Therefore, it's important to identify these early on and make an attempt to have them removed, or at least reduced. What are these charges? They go by many names but are usually fees for services for which you have already paid, don't need, or shouldn't have to pay for. For example, most escrow fees are all inclusive. That is, you pay a single fee that includes all normal escrow services. However, some escrow companies have taken to charging additional fees. These can include: document preparation, attorney's fees, and courier charges. Note that all of these describe services that may have been performed. However, preparation of documents (unless there was something unusual about your escrow) is done in the normal course of business. You shouldn't have to pay the escrow's attorney, unless you required special services. And unless your escrow required a special courier, these charges shouldn't be on there. And if they are, they should reflect the actual charges and not be marked up. Of course, there are many other potential "garbage fees." If you're not sure, ask your agent and/or your own attorney. You also may want to check out another informative source on the subject of closing the sale of a home, the *Home Closing Checklist*, also by Robert Irwin, 2003, McGraw-Hill. You may have to argue with your escrow officer to have these removed. Remember, if you didn't agree to pay them in your purchase agreement and your preliminary escrow instructions, you probably shouldn't have to.

Am I ready to sign the final escrow instructions?

There are usually two sets of escrow instructions. The preliminary instructions tell the escrow what to do. The final instructions are a kind of settlement report that tell you where the money's going and how much of it you'll get. (Included may be a copy of the HUD-1 settlement statement prepared for the buyer which describes in detail the final disposition of funds.) Everyone who's on the deed to the property normally will need to sign the final escrow instructions. And usually this will be done at the escrow company where the escrow officer can witness your signature(s). You'll also be asked to sign a deed to the buyer which will be held until the actual transfer of title takes place (usually a day or two later).

Have I contacted the escrow officer and set up a time for signing the final papers?

Typically your agent or the escrow officer will contact you telling you that you need to come down and sign the final papers. However, sometimes in the rush of things

people forget. If the time is near the expiration for closing
your transaction and you're aware that the buyer's loan
has been funded and all contingencies removed (you
have been tracking this, haven't you?!), you may want to
call the escrow officer yourself to find out when would be
a good time to come down. He or she will probably set
up a time within a few days. You'll go down, be presented
with the final closing instructions, and the deed to sign.
Until you (and the buyer) sign off, the deal can't close.

Will my agent and/or attorney be present?

It's a good idea to have your agent present since there may
be some questions you want to ask. For example, you'll
want to be sure that the commission is stated correctly and
that there are no additional transaction fees (unless you've
agreed to pay them). I've found that very often there are
unexpected charges to the seller in the final escrow
instructions that need to be explained. Unfortunately, the
escrow officer rarely will give you a detailed explanation,
sometimes for fear of being held liable for a mistatement.
For example, the charge may be for "additional title
search." What's that? The escrow officer may explain,
unhelpfully, that the title company has sent in an additional charge. Or the payoff demand from your lender
may be larger than you anticipated. The escrow officer
may explain, again unhelpfully, "That's what they sent
us." On the other hand, your agent may explain that there
was a cloud on the title which required additional
research, hence the added title search fee. Or the lender's
payoff demand included the last month's payment (which
you didn't pay) plus penalty. The agent can be very helpful here. Of course, if there's anything of a legal nature that
needs explanation, your attorney is the one to consult.

Do I understand all of the closing documents?

This is a question to ask yourself before signing. It goes
without saying that you should understand everything
you're being asked to sign. If there's something you don't
understand, if there are documents you think shouldn't be
there, if the figures don't add up, if a document is missing,
or if anything appears wrong, stop. Take a few moments
to ask the escrow officer questions. If you're still not satis-

fied, ask your agent or your attorney. Ignorance may be bliss, but it can be expensive. *Warning:* Do not unnecessarily hold up the close of escrow. It can result in an angry buyer and, if things go really badly, legal consequences.

Have I made all my moving plans?

Hopefully, you have thought about this already. Remember, you will need to give possession of the property to the buyers, typically at the close of escrow. That means that as soon as the deed is recorded in the buyers' favor, you need to be out of the property. Usually it's a good idea to contact the buyers (through their agent) to find out their plans regarding possession. Then you can coordinate. For example, most people like to move on a weekend. Thus, you might arrange to move out on a Saturday and they move in on a Sunday. Of course, this requires near split-second accuracy. If your movers are late or take longer than anticipated, confusion and conflict can result. Often, it's better to allow for a few days leeway, if possible. *Warning:* Sometimes for a wide variety of reasons, escrow doesn't close as anticipated. That means that you still own the house. If you move, you might need to move back. Even worse, if the new buyers have moved in, you might need to move them out! It's safest not to move until escrow has closed, the deed has transferred to the new buyers, and you've received your money.

Have I arranged for transfer of the key?

The symbolic transfer of ownership is when you present the buyers with the key to the house. Usually this is done by giving the key to your agent a few days before closing. Your agent may then hold it or pass it on to the buyers' agent with instructions not to give it to the buyers until the deal closes. Of course, you could just as easily give it directly to the buyers yourself, or make arrangements for them to pick it up. You should plan on giving the buyers *all* sets of keys that you have. After all, you won't have any need for them once the deal closes. However, keep in mind that any savvy buyer, while accepting your keys, will immediately have all the locks rekeyed as a security measure.

QUESTIONS TO ASK AN AGENT

Will you open escrow?

As soon as all parties sign the sales agreement, escrow
should be opened so that the closing can commence. It
really doesn't matter who opens escrow, as long as someone does. (There are issues of cost, and if you're paying,
you will want to look into finding the lowest priced
escrow service.) Usually your agent will do it, but call to
be sure. It may turn out that the buyer's agent is opening
escrow. Or neither agent is, in which case, to get the ball
rolling, you may want to do it yourself. (All that you need
is a copy of the sales agreement—take it in and an escrow
officer will begin the process.) The big mistake here is to
assume that someone else is doing it when they're not.
Call and find out.

Can I save money on title/escrow fees?

Your agent may know of a less expensive title/escrow company. By all means check them out. Also ask about a "reissue" fee. If it's only been a few years since you bought your
home, if you go back to the original title/escrow company,
they may be willing to give you a significantly reduced fee
(sometimes as much as a quarter or even a third off) for reis-
suing a policy of title insurance. Remember, however, that
the seller may not normally demand that the buyer use a
particular title insurance/escrow service. Note also that on
the East Coast sometimes attorneys will run the escrow and
that this is usually covered in their overall fee.

Will you check the abstract of title for me?

As soon as you open escrow, the escrow officer should
order an "abstract of title." This is a preliminary title
report that shows the chain of title to your property. It
also lists any liens, encumbrances, or other items that
cloud the title and may prevent you from selling. As soon
as it's available the escrow officer should call to let you
know. (Sometimes the call will be to your agent.) You can
then check it out. However, if you're unfamiliar with real
estate, looking over an abstract of title can be confusing.

Therefore, ask your agent (who presumably looks at these things on a regular basis), to check it out for you. Also, the title company will usually note any clouds on the title and your agent should be able to explain these. Getting clouds removed may require the services of an attorney.

Will you see to it that the buyers are removing contingencies?

You should ask this question early on. You want to be sure your agent is, indeed, keeping close tabs on the closing. You want to be reassured that he or she will regularly call the buyers' agent, and, sometimes, even the buyers themselves, to see what's happening. In most cases, however, it's simply a matter for the agent to keep checking with escrow to see that the appropriate documents are deposited in a timely fashion. Sometimes, however, your agent may candidly say that he or she simply doesn't have time to keep track of these things. The agent may be extremely busy, or may be leaving town on a business or pleasure trip. If that's the case, the agent should delegate this job to someone else in the office. Find out who this person is and stay on their back. In the rare case that the agent simply can't or won't track the escrow, you may need to do it yourself just to save the deal. The vast majority of agents, however, keep close track of escrow. After all, it's their money (in the commission), too.

Will you handle the "termite clearance"?

Remember, in order to sell, in most cases, you will need a termite clearance. That means calling up a pest/termite control company and arranging for an inspection. Then, you'll need to read the inspection and arrange for any repair and extermination work required to get the clearance. You should ask your agent if he or she will handle all of this for you. Most agents will. Indeed, they will prefer to do it just to be sure it's done in a timely fashion. (You'll still have to pay for it and sign that you agree to this.) However, if you have a lazy agent, then don't simply let things slide. Take it upon yourself to get this done. You can find pest/termite control companies on the Internet, in the Yellow Pages, and from recommendations by agents and friends.

Do you have disclosures for me to sign?

Your agent, presumably, knows which disclosures are required in your state and by the federal government. Most agents get them from their state or local Board of Realtors®, which prepares copies. Your agent should give these to you. In addition, he or she should explain what needs to be filled out and how to do it. However, the agent should *not* fill it out for you. These are your disclosures and you're really the only one who can answer the questions. *Note:* In many states the agent is likewise required to fill out a separate disclosure statement based on his or her observations of the property. If your agent can't or won't supply you with appropriate disclosures, check with an attorney or another agent. (Escrow companies will rarely supply these forms.) My suggestion is that you do not rely on forms that you may be able to buy at a local stationery store as they may or may not be appropriate for your area.

Has the buyer gotten approval for loan funding?

This is usually the most critical question in residential real estate closings. Unless and until the buyer secures his or her loan, the deal can't close. And your agent is the one to find out. Keep after your agent on this. It's the question you should ask of your agent each time you talk. Never mind that your agent is getting weary of your asking. It's critical to know. And if the agent discovers at any point along the way that the buyer won't be able to get a mortgage for any reason, it's time for you and your agent to plan on getting your house back on the market. (Remember, most buyers have a financing contingency in their purchase offer which allows them to back out of the deal, including keeping their deposit, if they can't get a needed mortgage.)

Will you attend the closing with me?

It's not that you need comfort, solace, or company. It's that you might have questions that your agent may be best equipped to answer. Of course, your end of the closing will probably only take a few minutes, so your agent should be able to be there. Nevertheless, many agents today would prefer not to attend. Agents who aren't attorneys can't give legal advice and they are worried that if they answer a question wrong, it could lead to a liability issue for them. Even so, impress upon your agent that you want him or her to be there. It should be part of the service that they perform for the commission they receive.

Are there any problems?

This is a catch-all question that you should ask whenever you see your agent. Hopefully, the response will be a solid, "Nope, things are going well." On the other hand, asking the question may encourage the agent to tell about something that he or she is afraid you won't want to hear. Nevertheless, better to get it out on the table as early as possible... so you can deal with whatever the problem may be.

12
Paying the Taxes

QUESTIONS TO ASK YOURSELF

Do I have to pay taxes when I sell my home? ☐

If you have a gain on the sale, then you may need to pay taxes on it. However, if you've lived in the house for 2 out of the past 5 years and it is your personal residence, up to $250,000 of that gain may be excluded from taxes (see below). If you do not meet the requirements for the exclusion and you've owned the property for at least a year, you may only be required to pay the capital gains tax on the gain. For periods shorter than a year, your gain will probably be combined with your personal income and you'll pay taxes on that.

Can I get a write-off if I sell my home for a loss? ☐

No. While a capital gain may be taxable (see above), a capital loss on your personal residence is not currently deductible.

Do I understand the difference between "profit" and "gain"? ☐

"Profit" is what you make on your home when you sell. For example, if you buy a home for $200,000, refinance for

Special Note: The author is not engaged in providing tax advice. The following is simply an overview of tax rules affecting real estate. For tax advice, consult with a tax professional.

$240,000 and later sell for $300,000, forgetting about transaction costs for the moment, many people would figure they made a profit of $60,000. They would simply subtract what they owe from what they received, in other words, their equity. "Gain," on the other hand, is a technical term used to calculate taxes you may owe on the sale of your property. Generally speaking, gain is what you paid for your property (or what it cost to build plus land). From this is subtracted certain costs such as casualty losses and added certain others such as improvements. This establishes a "basis" for tax purposes. Subtract this basis from the sale price, less transaction costs, and that is your gain. For example, if you paid $200,000 and later added a deck for $10,000, your basis might be $210,000. If you later sold for $300,000, after transaction costs, your gain would be $90,000. Notice that gain is calculated without regard to financing (or refinancing). It's also calculated without regard to equity.

Have I saved all my receipts?

When you sell, as noted above, you can add improvements that you made to your tax basis. Since the tax basis is subtracted from the sale price, the higher the basis, the lower the gain and, hence, the less tax to pay. You should have saved receipts for all improvements you made to your property to show to your accountant. *Note:* There's a difference between repair and maintenance and improvements. If you replace a broken water heater, you have not "improved" your property for tax purposes. On the other hand, if you add a new room, you have.

Will I have a capital gain on the sale of my property?

That's the big question most sellers want to know. After all, along with a capital gain often, though not necessarily (see below), come taxes. As noted above, you subtract your tax basis from the sale price (less costs) to determine if you have a capital gain. Unless you're quite good at doing taxes, however, I suggest you have your accountant do this calculation for you. It may seem simple, but when it comes to calculating basis it can get very tricky. You may want to make this calculation *before* you sell and use the result to make a decision on whether or not to sell.

Will I have a capital loss?

If your tax basis exceeds your sale price (after transaction costs), you probably have a capital loss. Unfortunately, as noted earlier, at this time a capital loss on the sale of your personal residence is not deductible. This feature of the IRS Code, however, will probably change eventually, so be sure to ask your accountant about it.

Who should I use as a tax advisor?

You should use someone who is competent and in whom you have confidence. This is usually an accountant, a certified public accountant (CPA), or a tax attorney. Sometimes real estate agents have advanced knowledge, certification, and degrees in the area of taxes and can double as both a broker and an accountant for you. Whomever you use, be sure that he or she knows what they're talking about. The last thing you want to do is to miscalculate your taxes and end up with penalties and late fees, or to overpay and spend more than you need.

Do I understand the tax exclusion on homes?

Introduced as part of the 1997 Tax Relief Act, it changed the tax code considerably. In the past you could "roll over" your taxable gain from your old home into your new one. That was done away with. Now, you may exclude up to $250,000 per individual (up to $500,000 per married couple) of your capital gain. The basic rules are that you must own the property and reside in it for 2 out of the past 5 years as your principle residence. In other words, if you meet the residence and time requirements, were you to sell and get a $275,000 gain, as a single person you could exclude $250,000. You would only need to pay tax on the $25,000 above the exclusion level. If you were a married couple, you could exclude the entire gain—pay no taxes on it at all. Of course, there are many small traps in the law. For example, your home must qualify as a residence, although most homes do, even if they are boathouses or mobile homes. And there are some plusses. If you can't meet the 2-year requirement and are forced to move because of illness or a job change, you may still be able to get a portion of the exclusion. Before assuming that you qualify, or don't qualify, check with your accountant.

What if I haven't lived in my home for the past 3 years?

The rule here is pretty straightforward. It's 2 out of the past 5 years. You may have moved out of your home and rented it for the past 3 years. But, if your accumulated time in the home as your principle residence has been at least 2 out of those 5 years, you probably will qualify. I say probably because recent tax court rulings have suggested that the interpretation of accumulated time may be made stricter in the future. Again, check with your accountant for recent tax code changes.

Is it my main residence?

This issue frequently comes up for people who own two homes, a main home and a vacation home. The exclusion applies only to your main home, the place where you spend most of your time. However, over the past 5 years you may have resided 2 years in your main home and 2 years in your vacation home. Therefore, depending on when you decide to sell, both may qualify. However, you can take the exclusion only once every 2 years.

Is my name on the title?

It's not good enough to just reside in the home. You must actually own it. In other words, your name should be on the title to the property. For homes with multiple owners, check with your accountant.

What if I recently converted the home from an investment property to my principal residence?

This is a technique that savvy investors have begun doing to legally avoid paying capital gains tax on their investment property. When you sell an investment property, the exclusion does not apply, hence there's tax to pay. However, you can convert an investment property to a principal residence by moving the tenants out and moving in yourself. Remember, however, that it's not just how long you own the property. You may have owned the property for 15 years as an investment. However, none of that counts toward the exclusion. You have to move in and then live there at least 2 years (out of 5) to get the exclusion.

Can I convert to an investment property and trade?

It is possible to go the other way. You can convert your personal residence to investment property by moving out yourself and renting it to tenants. As noted earlier, you can do this for 3 years, provided you previously resided in it for 2 years as your principle residence, and still claim the exclusion. But, if you rent it out for more than 3 years, you probably have lost the opportunity. Investment property, however, can be traded on a tax deferred basis (Section 1031). Again, see your accountant about this.

QUESTIONS TO ASK AN ACCOUNTANT

What is my adjusted tax basis?

Unless you understand accounting principles and the tax code quite well, my suggestion is that you ask a professional to determine what your tax basis is, adjusted upward and downward depending on improvements and losses. While you might come close, getting it exact can be tricky. You will need to know your adjusted basis in your house in order to subtract that figure from your sale price (after expenses of selling) in order to determine your capital gain or loss.

Do I qualify for the home exclusion?

It's the perfect question to ask your accountant. Present him or her with all the information about your residency and ownership and get an opinion. If you're not sure how the tax code works on this, getting a professional's opinion is well worth the cost.

Do you advise me to sell or hold and rent out my property?

While this decision is often made based on the housing market and your need to sell, it's also a good idea to consider it from an investment perspective. In recent years, homes have dramatically increased in value far outstripping stocks, bonds, and other investment avenues. Therefore, if you are contemplating selling, you should consult with your tax advisor to see if perhaps it would make good investment and tax sense to hold onto that property and rent it out. Remember, in today's marketplace, you don't necessarily need a large downpayment in order to buy a home. Often good credit is enough. Further, if you don't qualify for the 2-out-of-5-year exclusion, it might make more sense to hold and rent your house than to sell it. Again, this is a good question to ask your accountant.

Is there anything tax-wise that I'm overlooking?

Again, this is a general question to cover all the areas you may not have thought about. Don't assume you know all the answers. Don't even assume you know all the questions. When it's time to sell your home, check with your accountant for both specific and general advice.

Understanding the Terminology

If you're just getting introduced to real estate, you'll quickly realize that people in this field have a language all their own. There are points and disclosures and contingencies and dozens of other terms that can make you think people are talking in a foreign language.

Since buying a home is one of the biggest financial decisions in life, it's a good idea to become familiar with the following terms, which are frequently used in real estate. All too often a lack of understanding can result in very real consequences such as confusion and failure to act (or inappropriate action) on an important issue.

Abstract of Title: A written document produced by a title insurance company (in some states, an attorney will do it) giving the history of who owned the property from the first owner forward. It also indicates any liens or encumbrances that may affect the title. A lender will not make a loan, nor can a sale normally conclude, until the title to real estate is clear, as evidenced by the abstract.

Acceleration Clause: A clause that "accelerates" the payments in a mortgage, meaning that the entire amount becomes immediately due and payable. Most mortgages contain this clause (which kicks in if, for example, you sell the property).

Adjustable Rate Mortgage (ARM): A mortgage whose interest rate fluctuates according to an index and a margin agreed to in advance by both the borrower and lender.

Adjustment Date: The day on which an adjustment is made in an adjustable rate mortgage. It may occur monthly, every 6 months, once a year, or as otherwise agreed.

Agent: Any person licensed to sell real estate, whether a broker or a salesperson.

Alienation Clause: A clause in a mortgage specifying that if the property is transferred to another person, the mortgage becomes immediately due and payable. See also *Acceleration Clause.*

American Land Title Association (ALTA): A more complete and extensive policy of title insurance than most title insurance companies offer. It involves a physical inspection and often guarantees the property's boundaries. Lenders often insist on an ALTA policy, with themselves named as beneficiary.

American Society of Appraisers (ASA): A professional organization of appraisers.

Amortization: The repaying of the mortgage in equal installments. In other words, if the mortgage is for 30 years, you pay in 360 equal installments. (The last payment is often just a few dollars more or less than the rest of the payments. This is the opposite of a balloon payment schedule, by which one payment, usually the last one, is considerably larger than the rest.) See *Balloon Payment.*

Annual Percentage Rate (APR): The actual interest rate paid on a loan, including interest, loan fees, and points. The APR is determined by a government formula.

Appraisal: Valuation of a property, usually by a qualified appraiser, as required by most lenders. The amount of the appraisal is the maximum value on which the loan will be based. For example, if the appraisal is $100,000 and the lender loans 80 percent of value, the maximum mortgage will be $80,000.

As Is: A property sold without warrantees from the sellers. The sellers are essentially saying that they won't make any repairs. This does not, however, absolve them of the responsibility of making disclosures as to the condition of the property.

Assignment of Mortgage: The lender's sale of a mortgage usually not requiring the borrower's permission. For example, you may obtain a mortgage from XYZ Savings and Loan, which then sells the mortgage to Bland Bank. You will get a letter saying that the mortgage was reassigned and you are to make future payments to a new entity. The document used between lenders for the transfer is the assignment of mortgage.

Assumption: The taking over of an existing mortgage. For example, a seller may have an assumable mortgage on a property. When you buy the property, you take over that seller's obligation under the loan. Today, most fixed rate mortgages are not assumable. Most adjustable rate mortgages are assumable, but the borrower must qualify. FHA and VA mortgages may be assumable if certain conditions are met. When you assume the mortgage, you may be personally liable if there is a foreclosure.

Automatic Guarantee: The power assigned to some lenders to guarantee VA loans without first checking with the Veterans Administration. These lenders often can make the loans more quickly.

Backup: An offer that comes in after an earlier offer is accepted. If both buyer and seller agree, the backup assumes a secondary position to be acted on only if the original deal does not go through.

Balloon Payment: A single mortgage payment, usually the last, that is larger than all the others. In the case of second mortgages held by sellers, often only interest is paid until the due date—then the entire amount borrowed (the principal) is due. See *Second Mortgage*.

Biweekly Mortgage: A mortgage that is paid every other week instead of monthly. Since there are 52 weeks in the year, you end up making 26 payments, or the equivalent of 1 month's extra payment. The additional payments, applied to the principal, significantly reduce the amount of interest charged on the mortgage and often reduce the term of the loan.

Blanket Mortgage: A mortgage that covers several properties instead of a single property. It is used most frequently by developers and builders.

Broker: An independent licensed agent, one who can establish his or her own office. Salespeople, although they are licensed, must work for brokers, typically for a few years, to get enough experience to become fully licensed as independent brokers.

Buydown Mortgage: A mortgage with a lower-than-market interest rate, either for the entire term of the mortgage or for a set period at the beginning—say, 2 years. The buydown is made possible by the builder or seller paying an up-front fee to the lender.

Buyer's Agent: A real estate agent whose loyalty is to the buyer and not to the seller. Such agents are becoming increasingly common today.

Call Provision: A clause in a mortgage allowing the lender to call in the entire unpaid balance of the loan providing certain events have occurred, such as sale of the property. See also *Acceleration Clause.*

Canvass: To work a neighborhood; to go through it and knock on every door. Agents canvass to find listings. Investors and home buyers do it to find potential sellers who have not yet listed their property—and may agree to sell quickly for less.

Caps: Limits put on an adjustable rate mortgage. The interest rate, the monthly payment, or both may be capped.

Certificate of Reasonable Value (CRV): A document issued by the Veterans Administration establishing what the VA feels is the property's maximum value. In some cases, if a buyer pays more than this amount for the property, he or she will not get a VA loan.

Chain of Title: The history of ownership of the property. The title to property forms a chain going back to the first owners. In the Southwest, for example, the chain may start from the original Spanish land grants.

Closing: A meeting at which the seller conveys the title to the buyer and the buyer makes full payment to the seller, including financing, for the property. At the closing, all required documents are signed and delivered, and funds are disbursed. It also refers to the entire process of concluding a purchase.

Commission: The fee charged for an agent's services. Usually, but not always, the seller pays. There is no set fee; rather, the rate and amount is fully negotiable.

Commitment: A promise from the lender to the borrower offering a mortgage at a set amount, interest rate, and cost. Typically, commitments have a time limit—for example, they are good for 5 or 15 days. Some lenders charge for making a commitment if you don't subsequently take out the mortgage (since they have tied up the money for that amount of time). When the lender's offer is in writing, it is sometimes called a *firm commitment*.

Conforming Loan: A mortgage that complies fully with the underwriting requirements of Fannie Mae or Freddie Mac.

Construction Loan: A mortgage made for the purpose of constructing a building. The loan is written for a short term, typically under 12 months, and it is usually paid in installments directly to the builder as the work is completed. Most often, it is an interest-only loan.

Contingency: A condition that limits a contract. For example, the most common contingency says that a buyer is not required to complete a purchase if he or she fails to get necessary financing. See also *Subject To*.

Conventional Loan: Any loan that is not guaranteed or insured by the government.

Convertible Mortgage: An adjustable rate mortgage with a clause allowing it to be converted to a fixed rate mortgage (or the other way round) at some time in the future. You may have to pay an additional cost to obtain this type of mortgage.

Cosigner: Someone with better credit (usually a close relative) who agrees to sign your loan if by yourself you do not have a credit rating high enough to qualify for a mortgage (or the other way round). The cosigner is equally responsible for repayment of the loan. (If you don't pay it back, the cosigner may be held liable for the entire balance.)

Covenants, Conditions, and Restrictions (CC&Rs): Limits on the types of activities you as a property owner may engage in on the property. For example, you may be required to seek approval of a homeowners' association before adding on to your home or changing the color of the exterior. Or you may be restricted from adding a second or third story to your home.

Credit Report: A report, usually from one of the country's three large credit reporting companies, that gives your credit history. It typically lists all your delinquent payments or failures to pay as well as any bankruptcies and, sometimes, foreclosures. Lenders use the report to determine whether to offer you a mortgage. The fee for obtaining the report is usually under $50, and you typically are charged for it.

Deal Point: A point on which the deal hinges. It can be as important as the price or as trivial as changing the color of the mailbox.

Deposit: The money that buyers put up (also called *earnest money*) to demonstrate their seriousness in making an offer. The deposit is usually at risk if the buyers fail to complete the transaction and have no acceptable way of backing out of the deal. This is not to be confused with the down payment, which is the difference between the amount financed and the purchase price.

Disclosures: A list and explanation of the features and defects in a property that sellers give to buyers. Also a list and explanation of the terms and conditions in a contract such as a mortgage instrument. Most states now require disclosures.

Discount: The amount that a lender withholds from a mortgage to cover the points and fees. For example, you may borrow $100,000, but your points and fees come to $3000; hence the lender will fund only $97,000, discounting the $3000. Also, in the secondary market, a discount is the amount less than face value that a buyer of a mortgage pays in order to be induced to take out the loan. The discount here is calculated on the basis of risk, market rates, interest rate of the note, and other factors. See *Points.*

Dual Agent: An agent who expresses loyalty to both buyers and sellers and agrees to work with both. Only a few agents can successfully play this role.

Due-on-Encumbrance Clause: A little noted and seldom-enforced clause in some recent mortgages that allows the lender to foreclose if the borrower gets additional financing.

For example, if you secure a second mortgage, the lender of the first mortgage may have grounds for foreclosing. The reasoning here is that if you reduce your equity level by taking out additional financing, the lender may be placed in a less secure position.

Due-on-Sale Clause: A clause in a mortgage specifying that the entire unpaid balance becomes due and payable on sale of the property. See *Acceleration Clause.*

Escrow Company: An independent third party (stakeholder) that handles funds; carries out the instructions of the lender, buyer, and seller in a transaction; and deals with all the documents. In most states, companies are licensed to handle escrows. In some parts of the country, particularly the Northeast, the function of the escrow company may be handled by an attorney.

FHA Loan: A mortgage insured by the Federal Housing Administration. In most cases, the FHA advances no money but instead insures the loan to a lender such as a bank. There is a fee to the borrower, usually paid up front, for this insurance.

Fixed-Rate Mortgage: A mortgage whose interest rate does not fluctuate for the life of the loan.

Fixer-Upper: A home that does not show well and is in bad shape. Often the property is euphemistically referred to in listings as a "TLC" (needs tender loving care) or "handyman's special."

Foreclosure: Legal proceeding in which the lender takes possession and title to a property, usually after the borrower fails to make timely payments on a mortgage.

Fannie Mae: Any of the publicly traded securities collateralized by a pool of mortgages backed by the Federal National Mortgage Association. A secondary lender.

Freddie Mac: A publicly traded security collateralized by a pool of mortgages backed by the Federal Home Loan Mortgage Corporation. A secondary lender.

FSBO: For sale by owner.

Garbage Fees: Extra (and often unwarranted) charges tacked on when a buyer obtains a mortgage.

Graduated-Payment Mortgage: A mortgage whose payments vary over the life of the loan. The payments start out low, then slowly rise until, usually after a few years, they reach a plateau where they remain for the balance of the term. Such a mortgage is particularly useful when you want low initial payments. It is primarily used by first-time buyers, often in combination with a fixed-rate or adjustable rate mortgage.

Growing Equity Mortgage: A rarely used mortgage whose payments increase according to a set schedule. The purpose is to pay additional money into principal and thus pay off the loan earlier and save interest charges.

Homeowners' Association (HOA): An organization found mainly in condominium complexes but also in some single-family areas. It represents homeowners and establishes and maintains neighborhood architectural and other standards. You usually must get permission from the HOA to make significant external changes to your property.

Index: A measurement of an established interest rate used to determine the periodic adjustments for adjustable rate mortgages. There is a wide variety of indexes, including the Treasury bill rates and the cost of funds to lenders.

Inspection: A physical survey of the property to determine if there are any problems or defects.

Jumbo Mortgage: A mortgage for more than the maximum amount of a *Conforming Loan*.

Lien: A claim for money against real estate. For example, if you had work done on your property and refused to pay the worker, he or she might file a *mechanic's lien* against your property. If you didn't pay taxes, the taxing agency might file a *tax lien*. These liens "cloud" the title and usually prevent you from selling the property or refinancing it until they are cleared by paying off the debt.

Loan-to-Value Ratio (LTV): The percentage of the appraised value of a property that a lender will loan. For example, if your property appraises at $100,000 and the lender is willing to loan $80,000, the loan-to-value ratio is 80 percent.

Lock In: To tie up the interest rate for a mortgage in advance of actually getting the loan. For example, a buyer might lock in a mortgage at 7.5 percent so that if rates subsequently rose, he or she would still get that rate. Sometimes there's a fee for this. It's always a good idea to get it in writing from the lender, just to be sure that if rates rise, the lender doesn't change its mind.

Low-Ball: To make a very low initial offer to purchase.

Margin: An amount, calculated in points, that a lender adds to an index to determine how much interest you will pay during a period for an adjustable rate mortgage. For example, the index may be at 7 percent, and the margin agreed upon at the time you obtain the mortgage may be 2.7 points. The interest rate for that period, therefore, is 9.7 percent. See also *Index, Points.*

Median Sales Price: The midpoint of the price of homes. As many properties have sold above this price as have sold below it.

Member, American Institute of Real Estate Appraisers (MAI): An appraiser who has completed rigorous training and has qualified for this title.

Mortgage: A loan arrangement between a borrower, or *mortgagor,* and a lender, or *mortgagee.* If you don't make your payments on a mortgage, the lender can foreclose, or take ownership of the property, only by going to court. This court action can take a great deal of time, often 6 months or more. Further, even after the lender has taken back the property, you may have an *equity of redemption* that allows you to redeem the property for years afterward, by paying back the mortgage and the lender's costs. The length of time it takes to foreclose, the costs involved, and the equity of redemption make a mortgage much less desirable to lenders than a *Trust Deed.*

Mortgage Banker: A lender that specializes in offering mortgages but none of the other services normally provided by a bank.

Mortgage Broker: A person or company that specializes in providing "retail" mortgages to consumers. It usually represents many different lenders.

Motivated Seller: A seller who has a strong desire to sell. For example, the seller may have been transferred and must move quickly.

Multiple Counteroffers: Comeback offers extended by the seller to several buyers simultaneously.

Multiple Listing Service (MLS): A local service used by Realtors® as a listings exchange. Nearly 90 percent of all homes listed in the country are found on the MLS.

Multiple Offers: Offers submitted simultaneously from several buyers for the same property.

Negative Amortization: A condition arising when the payment on an adjustable rate mortgage is not sufficiently large to cover the interest charged. The excess interest is then added to the principal so the amount borrowed actually increases. The amount that the principal can increase is usually limited to 125 percent of the original mortgage value. Any mortgage that includes payment *Caps* has the potential to be negatively amortized.

Origination Fee: An expense in obtaining a mortgage. Originally, it was a charge that lenders made for preparing and submitting a mortgage. The fee applied only to FHA and VA loans, which had to be submitted to the government for approval. With an FHA loan, the maximum origination fee was 1 percent.

Personal Property: Any property that does not go with the land. Such property includes automobiles, clothing, and most furniture. Some items such as appliances and floor and wall coverings are disputable. See also *Real Property*.

Points: A point is 1 percent of a mortgage amount, payable on obtaining the loan. For example, if your mortgage is $100,000 and you are required to pay 2 ½ points to get it, the charge to you is $2500. Some points may be tax deductible. Check with your accountant. A *basis point* is 1/100 of a point. For example, if you are charged ½ point (0.5 percent of the mortgage), the lender may refer to it as "50 basis points."

Preapproval: Formal approval for a mortgage from a lender. You have to submit a standard application and have a credit check. Also, the lender may require proof of income, employment, and money on deposit (to be used for the downpayment and closing costs).

Prepayment Penalty: A charge demanded by the lender from the borrower for paying off a mortgage early. In times past (more than 25 years ago), nearly all mortgages carried prepayment penalties. However, those mortgages were also assumable by others. Today virtually no fixed-rate mortgages (other than FHA or VA mortgages) are truly assumable; however, some carry a prepayment penalty clause. See *Assumption*.

Principal, Interest, Taxes, and Insurance (PITI): These are the major components that go into determining the monthly payment on a mortgage. (Other items include homeowners' association dues and utilities.)

Private Mortgage Insurance (PMI): Insurance that protects the lender in the event that the borrower defaults on a mortgage. It is written by an independent third-party insurance company and typically covers only the first 20 percent of the lender's potential loss. PMI is normally required on any mortgage that exceeds an 80 percent loan-to-value ratio.

Purchase Money Mortgage: A mortgage obtained as part of the purchase price of a home (usually from the seller) as opposed to a mortgage obtained through refinancing. In some states, no deficiency judgment can be obtained against the borrower of a purchase money mortgage. (That is, if there is a foreclosure and the property brings less than the amount borrowed, the borrower cannot be held liable for the shortfall.)

Real Estate Owned (REO): Property taken back through foreclosure and held for sale by a lender.

Real Estate Settlement Procedures Act (RESPA): Legislation requiring lenders to provide borrowers with specific information on the cost of securing financing. Basically it means that before you proceed too far along the path of getting the mortgage, the lender has to provide you with an estimate of costs.

Real Property: Real estate. This includes the land and anything appurtenant to it, including the house. Certain tests have been devised to determine whether an item is real property (goes with the land). For example, if curtains or draperies have been attached in such a way that they cannot be removed without damaging the home, they may be considered real property. But if they can easily be removed without damaging the home, they may be personal property. The purchase agreement should specify whether questionable items are real or personal to avoid confusion later on.

REALTOR®: A broker who is a member of the National Association of REALTORS. Agents who are not members may not use the REALTOR designation.

Second Mortgage: An inferior mortgage usually placed on the property after a first mortgage. In the event of foreclosure, the second mortgage is paid off only if and when the first mortgage has been fully paid. Many lenders will not offer second mortgages.

Short Sale: Property sale in which a lender agrees to accept less than the mortgage amount in order to facilitate the sale and avoid a foreclosure.

Society of Real Estate Appraisers (SREA): A professional association to which qualified appraisers can belong.

Subject To: A contingency. Also a phrase often used to indicate that a buyer is not assuming the mortgage liability of a seller. For example, if the seller has an assumable loan and the buyer assumes the loan, he or she is taking over liability for payment. On the other hand, if you purchase subject to the mortgage, you do not assume liability for payment.

Subordination Clause: A clause in a mortgage document that keeps the mortgage subordinate to another mortgage.

Title: Legal evidence that you actually have the right of ownership of *Real Property*. It is given in the form of a deed (there are many different types of deeds) that specifies the kind of title you have (joint, common, or other).

Title Insurance Policy: An insurance policy that covers the title to a home. It may list the owner or the lender as beneficiary. The policy is issued by a title insurance company and specifies that if for any covered reason your title proves defective, the company will correct the title or compensate you up to a specified amount, usually the amount of the purchase price or the mortgage. *Note:* Title insurance offers protection for problems that occurred prior to your taking ownership, not after (even though the problem may be discovered later.)

Trust Deed: A three-party lending arrangement that includes a borrower, or *trustor*; an independent third-party stakeholder, or *trustee* (usually a title insurance company); and a lender, or *beneficiary*, so called because the lender stands to benefit if the trustee turns the deed over in case the borrower fails to make payments. The advantage to the lender of the trust deed over the mortgage is that foreclosure can be accomplished without court action. Usually there can be no deficiency judgment against the borrower. (In other words, if the property is worth less than the loan, the lender can't come back to the borrower after the sale for the difference.) See also *Purchase Money Mortgage.*

Upgrade: Any extra that a buyer may obtain when purchasing a new home—for example, a better-quality carpet or a wall mirror in the bedroom.

Upside Down: Owing more on a property than its market value.

VA Loan: A mortgage guaranteed by the U.S. Department of Veterans Affairs (VA). The VA actually guarantees only a small percentage of the loan amount, but since it guarantees the "top" of the monies loaned, lenders are willing to accept the arrangement. In a VA loan the government advances no money; rather, the mortgage is made by a private lender such as a bank.

Wraparound Financing: A blend of two mortgages, often used by sellers to get a higher interest rate or facilitate a sale. For example, instead of giving a buyer a simple *Second Mortgage,* the seller may combine the balance due on an existing mortgage (usually an existing first) with an additional loan. Thus the wrap includes both the second and the first mortgages. The borrower makes payments to the seller, who then keeps part of the payment and in turn pays off the existing mortgage.

Internet Resources

Robert Irwin, www.robertirwin.com   The author's Web site.

GOVERNMENT AGENCIES

U.S. Department of Housing and Urban Development (HUD), www.hud.gov   Information on government programs including those involving settlement/closing procedures.

Federal Housing Administration (FHA), http://www.hud.gov/offices/hsg/index.cfm   Information on FHA loan insurance and housing programs.

U.S. Department of Veterans Affairs (VA), www.va.gov   Information on VA loan guarantees and housing programs.

SECONDARY LENDERS

Fannie Mae, www.fanniemae.com and *www.homepath.com*   Loans, settlement procedures, and foreclosures.

Freddie Mac, www.freddiemac.com   Information on loans and settlement procedures.

Ginnie Mae, www.ginniemae.gov   Information on home purchasing and ownership.

CREDIT BUREAUS AND ORGANIZATIONS

Consumer Data Industry Associations, http://www.cdiaonline.org/   Information on credit reports and credit laws.

Equifax, www.equifax.com   National credit reporting agency.

Experian, www.experian.com   National credit reporting agency.

Fair Isaac (credit scores), www.fairisaac.com   Main credit scoring organization.

Federal Trade Commission, www.ftc.gov   Handles credit reporting complaints.

Trans Union, www.transunion.com   National credit reporting agency.

TITLE INSURANCE/ESCROW ORGANIZATIONS

ALTA form, www.alta.org/store/forms/homeown.pdf   Provides the basic form for ALTA policies.

American Escrow Association, http://www.a-e-a.org   A major escrow trade association.

American Land Title Associations, www.alta.org   A major title association trade association.

California Escrow Association, www.ceaescrow.org   California's trade escrow association.

California Land Title Association, www.alta.org/store/forms/ homeown.pdf   California's trade title association.

Chicago Title Insurance Company, www.ctic.com   A major title insurance company.

First American Title Insurance Company, http://firstam.com   Major title insurance company.

Illinois Land Title Association, www.illinoislandtitle.org   The Illinois trade title insurance association.

Texas Land Title Association, www.tlta.com   The Texas trade title insurance association.

HOME INSPECTION ORGANIZATIONS

American Institute of Inspectors, www.inspection.org   A home inspection trade association.

American Society of Home Inspectors, www.ashi.com   The largest national home inspection trade association.

National Association of Certified Home Inspectors, www.nachi. org   The national home inspector trade association.

OTHER RELATED ORGANIZATIONS

Dataquick, www.dataquick.com   Provides information on real estate (fee).

National Association of Realtors, www.realtor.com, www.realtor.org Provides information on members, homes for sale, and other data.

The legal description, www.thelegaldescription.com Provides information on legal news regarding home closings.

Index

About the Author

Robert Irwin, one of America's leading experts in all areas of real estate, is the author of more than 40 books, including McGraw-Hill's best-selling Tips and Traps series and *Home Renovation Checklist*. For more real estate tips and traps, go to www.robertirwin.com.